Contents

• •

The variety of activities in this book will strengthen your students' thinking skills and enhance their learning. The lessons provide practice in:

Thinking Creatively
fluency, flexibility, original ideas, mental imagery, problem solving

Thinking Logically
analogies, generalizing, patterning, comparing and contrasting, deductive reasoning, problem solving

Thinking Critically
ordering, classifying, analyzing, evaluating, observing, comparing and contrasting, problem solving

• •

Overview

Charts

In *Thinking Skills,* 44 charts pose questions that engage students in problem-solving activities. Order the lessons to meet the needs of your students. Downloadable, interactive charts that bring the lessons to life are also available. (See page 3 for download instructions.) So whether you choose the chart provided in this book or the animated, downloadable version, your students will be participating in activities that strengthen their thinking skills.

Teacher Pages

For each chart, an accompanying teacher's page provides guidelines for modeling and practicing critical-, logical-, and creative-thinking strategies. As you conduct these lessons, encourage students to explain the thinking behind their responses. Accept all answers that can be logically substantiated. Encourage thinking "outside the box" or using a unique perspective.

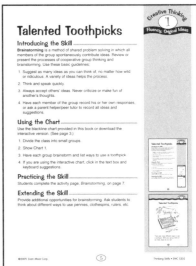

Reproducible Practice Activities

A reproducible student page is included for each of the 44 lessons. These pages extend the thinking skill focused on in each lesson. They are useful as whole-class activities or as independent practice.

Downloadable Interactive Charts

You Get 44 Animated Charts

The 44 charts in this book are presented in full color with an interactive element that will engage students in the thinking activities. Connect your computer to a projection system to present a whole-class lesson. As an independent activity, students may view charts on a classroom computer to assist them in completing the reproducible practice activities.

How to Download:

1. Go to evan-moor.com/resources.
2. Enter your e-mail address and the resource code for this product—EMC5302. Important: You **must** provide a valid e-mail to access the content.
3. You will receive an e-mail with a link to the downloadable charts.
4. Download the file and follow the instructions in the readme.txt file included with the install package.

Steps for Use

Use the interactive software to introduce each topic. After brainstorming possibilities, utilize the interactive elements described on the teacher page to answer each question.

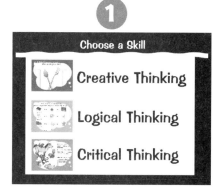

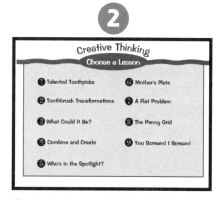

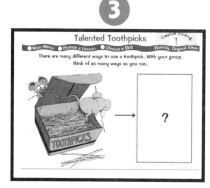

Click on **Choose a Skill** to display the list of categories. Click on the category of thinking skill you wish to introduce or practice.

Select a lesson number.

The chart will be displayed. Each chart provides an interactive element to help students think about the topic.

Thinking Skills • EMC 5302

Creative Thinking

Talented Toothpicks

Introducing the Skill

Brainstorming is a method of shared problem solving in which all members of the group spontaneously contribute ideas. Review or present the processes of cooperative group thinking and brainstorming. Use these basic guidelines:

1. Suggest as many ideas as you can think of, no matter how wild or ridiculous. A variety of ideas helps the process.

2. Think and speak quickly.

3. Always accept others' ideas. Never criticize or make fun of another's thoughts.

4. Have each member of the group record his or her own responses, or ask a parent helper/peer tutor to record all ideas and suggestions.

Using the Chart

Use the blackline chart provided in this book or download the interactive version. (See page 3.)

1. Divide the class into small groups.

2. Show Chart 1.

3. Have each group brainstorm and list ways to use a toothpick.

4. If you are using the interactive chart, click in the text box and keyboard suggestions.

Practicing the Skill

Students complete the activity page, *Brainstorming,* on page 7.

Extending the Skill

Provide additional opportunities for brainstorming. Ask students to think about different ways to use pennies, clothespins, rulers, etc.

Talented Toothpicks

There are many different ways to use a toothpick. With your group, think of as many ways as you can.

Thinking Skills • EMC 5302

Name _____

Brainstorming

List all the things you can do with a straw.
Think of as many as you can.

_____

_____

_____

_____

_____

_____

_____

_____

_____

_____

_____

Thinking Skills • EMC 5302

Toothbrush Transformations

Introducing the Skill

1. **Transforming** something means to markedly change the form or appearance of something. When students transform objects, it allows them to show their creative and spontaneous sides. Ask students to think of ways that something might be transformed. Record their ideas.

2. Share any ideas on the following list that students have not mentioned. Post your complete list for student reference.

   • Change its color and form.

   • Enlarge it or reduce it.

   • Change its odor, sound, or feel.

   • Add or subtract strength.

   • Rearrange the parts. Change its pattern.

   • Reverse it. Draw it backward or upside down.

   • Combine it with other materials or objects.

Using the Chart

Use the blackline chart provided in this book or download the interactive version. (See page 3.)

1. Show Chart 2.

2. Have each student draw the toothbrush transformed in several different ways and list uses for each new transformation.

3. If you are using the interactive chart, click on a question mark. Read one suggested change and discuss ways to make that change. Repeat with another question.

Practicing the Skill

Students complete the activity page, *Transforming,* on page 10.

Extending the Skill

1. Choose a familiar classroom object.

2. Challenge students to transform the object and think of new uses.

3. Create a class book, binding all of the students' responses together.

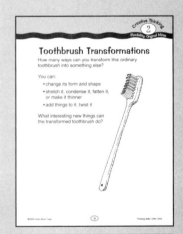

Toothbrush Transformations

How many ways can you transform this ordinary toothbrush into something else?

You can:

- change its form and shape
- stretch it, condense it, fatten it, or make it thinner
- add things to it, twist it

What interesting new things can the transformed toothbrush do?

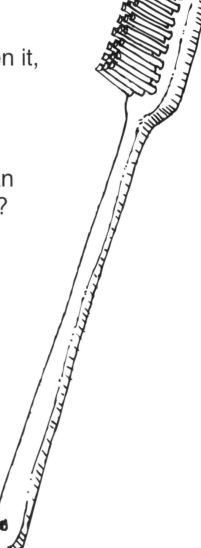

Name _____

Transforming

Choose one of the pictured objects and transform it so that it can be used in each of the four functions named in the boxes below.

Draw a picture of the transformed object in each box and explain how it can be used to accomplish its function. List **all** ideas on the back of this paper.

play a tune	be the main piece in a new game
clean the chalkboard	kill weeds

What Could It Be?

Introducing the Skill

Help students to exercise **mental flexibility**. Like any stretching routine, the first few times are the most difficult. Encourage students to stick with the "stretch," and in a short time they'll develop momentum. Then one idea will trigger the next.

Using the Chart

Use the blackline chart provided in this book or download the interactive version. (See page 3.)

1. Show Chart 3.

2. Explain that pondering the shapes on the chart may lead to curious and unusual interpretations. (For example, students might see the first shape as a beach ball, a pie divided for four hungry eaters, the cross hairs on a periscope, a bird's-eye view of an intersection, or the top of a beanie. All of the responses are correct.)

3. Have each student think of at least three interpretations for each shape on the chart. If you are using the interactive chart, click in the text box by a figure. Keyboard possible names for it. Repeat for each figure.

Practicing the Skill

Students complete the activity page, *Five Ways,* on page 13.

Extending the Skill

Apply mental flexibility to real classroom problems and see what solutions develop. For example:

- Think of five ways to speed up the line in the lunchroom.

- Think of five ways to have more free time.

- Think of five ways to help new students feel welcome.

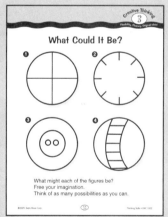

What Could It Be?

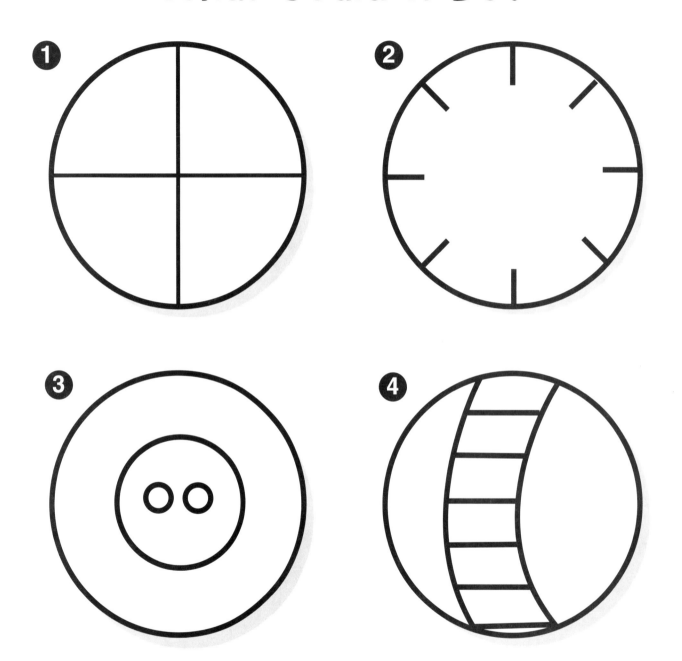

What might each of the figures be?
Free your imagination.
Think of as many possibilities as you can.

Thinking Skills • EMC 5302

Five Ways

Think of five ways to be a better student.
List your ideas here.

1. _____

_____

2. _____

_____

3. _____

_____

4. _____

_____

5. _____

_____

Thinking Skills • EMC 5302

Combine and Create

Introducing the Skill

Mental flexibility allows you to look at familiar objects with new perspectives and to combine two individual objects to make one new object for a new purpose.

Using the Chart

Use the blackline chart provided in this book or download the interactive version. (See page 3.)

1. Show Chart 4.

2. Have students explain the attributes of a spoon. Record them on a chart or the chalkboard. If you are using the interactive chart, click in each text box and record the attributes.

   It scoops.
   It divides.
   It measures.
   It scrapes.

3. Have students explain the attributes of a fork.

   It spears.
   It lifts.
   It holds something in place.
   It tears.

4. Have students draw a combination of the two utensils. *(a spoon-fork, a spork, or a foon)* Combine the attributes and list them.

   It scoops and spears.
   It divides and lifts.
   It measures and holds something in place.
   It scrapes and tears.

Practicing the Skill

Students complete the activity page, *What Will It Be?,* on page 16.

Extending the Skill

1. Have students choose two familiar classroom objects and combine them.

2. Ask students to draw the combination and list the attributes of the new combination.

Combine and Create

What could you make?

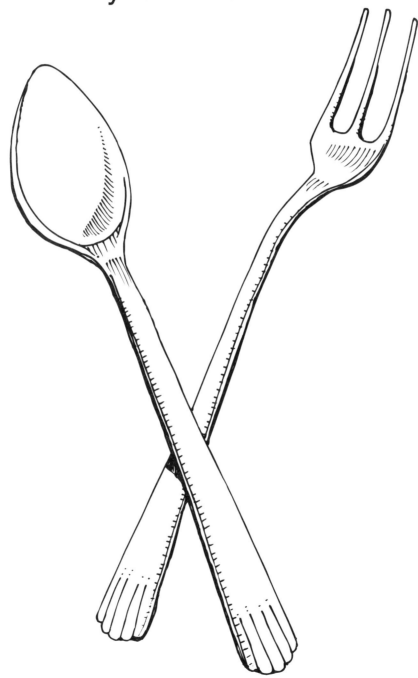

What Will It Be?

Choose two of the items shown.
Combine them in a new invention.

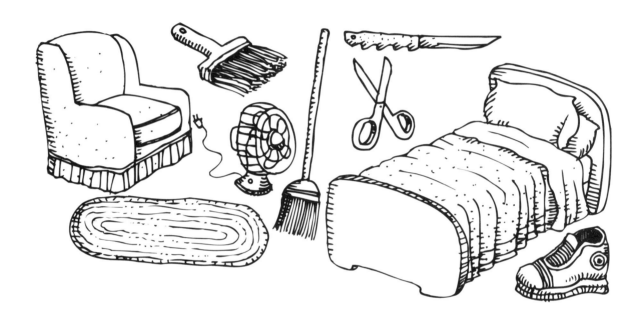

- **What items will you combine?**

_____ and _____

- **What does your invention do?**

_____

- **Who will use it?**

_____

Thinking Skills • EMC 5302

Who's in the Spotlight?

Introducing the Skill

Imaging not only teaches students to focus on visual representations, but also improves their ability to think on a multisensory level. Spend a moment having students close their eyes and letting their minds concentrate on various situations that you suggest. Have students pretend that their eyelids are homemade movie screens. Whatever they visualize will be shown in color on their screen.

Using the Chart

Use the blackline chart provided in this book or download the interactive version. (See page 3.)

1. Tell students that they are going to picture in their mind's eye an image that you will describe.

2. Show Chart 5. Read the description as students create a mental picture. Have students share their ideas with the class.

3. If you are using the interactive chart, click in the spotlights to find answers to the questions.

Practicing the Skill

1. Read the following description to students. Ask them to create a mental picture of the object described.

   Think of a large triangle that has all sides of equal length. In the top corner of the triangle is a small circle. Across the top of the circle are four curved lines that look like eyelashes. In the bottom right-hand corner is a flower with four petals and two leaves on the stem. In the left-hand corner of the triangle is another circle. In the middle of the circle is a square. In the middle of the square is a large dot.

2. Have students draw the figure on the top part of the activity page, *In Your Mind's Eye,* on page 19.

Extending the Skill

1. Have students complete the second half of the activity page. They will choose a familiar object and write a description.

2. Then have students read their description to a friend and ask him or her to draw the object.

Who's in the Spotlight?

Use your "mind's eye" to see a picture.

Hear a pipe organ quickly play a lively tune. Listen to people laughing and clapping.

Hear the sounds of an elephant's trumpet and a lion's roar. A sharp cracking sound rips through the air nearby.

Smell the scent of newly mowed hay mixed with mouthwatering aromas of popcorn and peanuts.

Watch a man step forward into a circle of light.

He's wearing big, baggy pants; a dark shirt; and a wide, polka-dotted tie. His shoes are three times the normal size, and a small black hat sits cockeyed on his head.

His huge nose is as red as an apple. His painted mouth is turned down at the corners. He carries a small broom and begins to sweep at the edges of the light. People begin to giggle.

Where are you?

Who is the man in the circle of light?

Thinking Skills • EMC 5302

Name _____

In Your Mind's Eye

In the box, draw the object your teacher described.

Choose an object and write a paragraph describing it, but not naming it. Include descriptions of the sounds, smells, and feelings associated with the object. Read your description to a classmate. See if that person can draw the object from your description.

_____

_____

_____

_____

_____

Mother's Plate

Introducing the Skill

1. Reproduce a symbol familiar to your students, such as your school logo.

2. Cut the reproduced symbol into five pieces. Rotate the pieces and display them for students to view.

3. Ask them to use their mind's eye to rotate and put the pieces back together to identify the symbol.

4. Actually put the pieces together.

Using the Chart

Use the blackline chart provided in this book or download the interactive version. (See page 3.)

1. Show Chart 6.

2. Have students visualize the completed plate. After students have rotated the pieces in their heads, you may use the interactive chart and click on each piece to put it together.

3. Be sure to take time to discuss how various individuals approached the problem.

Practicing the Skill

1. Students complete the activity page, *The Broken Plate,* on page 22.

2. Store students' puzzles in envelopes to use as a free-time activity.

Extending the Skill

Provide a variety of jigsaw puzzles for students to put together.

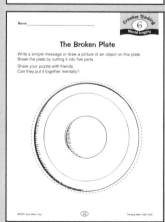

Mother's Plate

Celia dropped the plate that she had made for her mother. It broke into five pieces. Study the pieces and put them back together in your head. Can you figure out the message that Celia painted on the plate?

 Thinking Skills • EMC 5302

Name _____

The Broken Plate

Write a simple message or draw a picture of an object on this plate.
Break the plate by cutting it into five parts.

Share your puzzle with friends.
Can they put it together mentally?

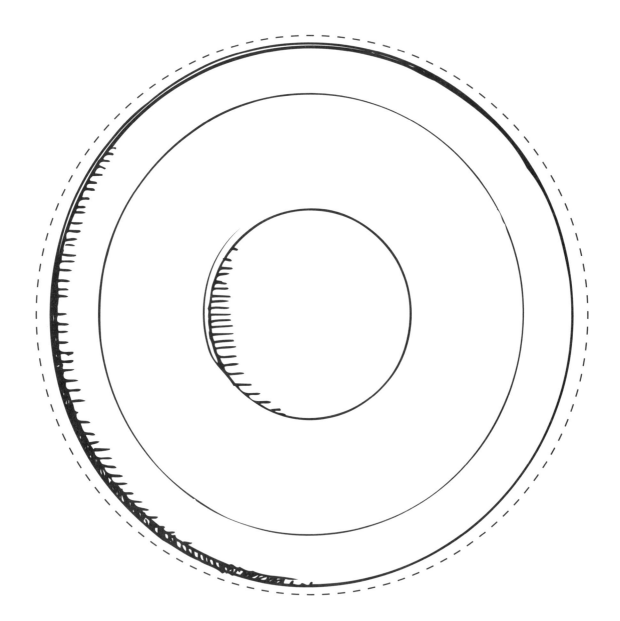

Thinking Skills • EMC 5302

A Flat Problem

Introducing the Skill

Discuss with students their experiences riding a school bus. Share any anxious or unusual moments.

Using the Chart

Use the blackline chart provided in this book or download the interactive version. (See page 3.)

1. Show Chart 7.

2. Read the following situation to your students:

   Imagine that you are on your way to school in a school bus. The driver has just picked up all the children at the last stop before arriving at the school. As the bus slowly begins to roll down the road, you hear a loud thumping sound coming from the bottom of the bus. The driver pulls off the road and gets out to check. When she tries to get back on the bus, the door sticks and will not open. She decides to go for help.

3. Give students several minutes to imagine the scene on the bus. Tell them to imagine the sights, sounds, and smells associated with the scene.

4. Ask students to answer the following questions:

   • *Who will take charge on the bus?*
   • *What do all the students on the bus do while they're waiting?*
   • *What happens when the bus driver returns?*

5. Encourage students to share what they think will happen in the end. If you are using the interactive chart, click in the text box to keyboard the conclusion of this story.

Practicing the Skill

Students complete the activity page, *Picture This,* on page 25.

Extending the Skill

1. Pose a situation that might occur in the classroom. For example:

   • *The paint spills in the art center.*
   • *The teacher is late picking up the class after lunch.*

2. Have students imagine the situation and suggest possible solutions.

3. Set up guidelines based on students' suggestions.

A Flat Problem

Listen to the story that goes with this picture.
Picture the events in your mind.
What do you see happening?

Thinking Skills • EMC 5302

Name _____

 **Picture This**

Circle one of the situations below: **1**, **2**, or **3**.
Close your eyes and imagine the scene.
What is happening to you?
Write your description of the situation on the lines below.

1. You are by yourself in the middle of a large forest. The sunlight is streaming down through the trees, and leaves crunch under your feet as you walk. You are tired, so you sit and rest on the mossy floor in a little clearing. Suddenly, you hear a rustling sound in a small bush nearby.

2. You are in the supermarket with your mother. You are pushing the cart while she loads it with items your family needs. See the vegetable and meat cases, and the brightly colored boxes and cans in each aisle. As you turn the last corner, there suddenly looms a large display of canned soups that you did not see.

3. You are the first student in your new classroom at school. The air is full of the smell of chalk dust and new books. You feel stiff and uncomfortable with your new school clothes on. As other students begin to file in, you can hear the sounds of their shoes shuffling by your desk quietly. Suddenly, you look up and see a wonderful sight!

_____

_____

_____

_____

The Penny Grid

Introducing the Skill

Brainteasers are to the mind as what stretching is to the body. Both develop flexibility.

Using the Chart

Use the blackline chart provided in this book or download the interactive version. (See page 3.)

1. Show Chart 8.

2. Give students time to work out a solution.

3. If you are using the interactive chart, click on individual squares to divide the chart into two equal parts by changing the background color. Click again to change a square back to white.

Practicing the Skill

Students complete the activity page, *The Cake,* on page 28.

Extending the Skill

Post a brainteaser daily. Take time at the end of the day to discuss possible solutions and the process students used to solve the problems. Here are three to get you started:

1. Begin with the letter *I*. Imagine a continuous line from letter to letter that creates a meaningful sentence. It can go left, right, up, or down, but never diagonally. You can use every letter only once. You must use every letter.

E	H	A	E
W	T	D	ER NA
O	R	I	N
S	D	C	A

   Answer: I can read the words.

2. Arrange the four initial letters of *north, south, east,* and *west* so that they spell something that comes to us every day from all directions.

   Answer: news

3. Place the same number in all four corners so that both outer columns add up to 21.

☐	5	4	☐
8			2
1			7
☐	9	0	☐

   Answer: 6 goes in each corner.

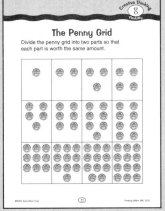

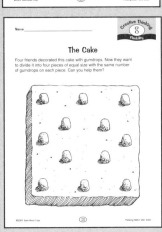

The Penny Grid

Divide the penny grid into two parts so that each part is worth the same amount.

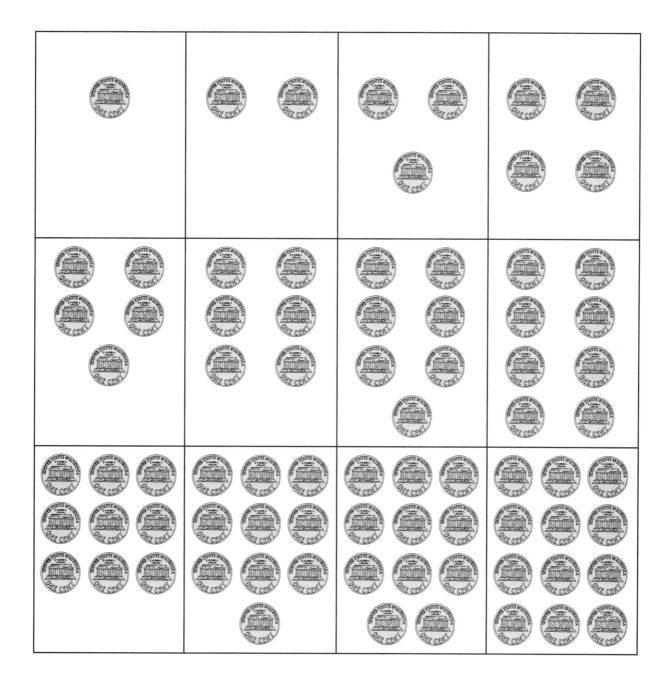

Thinking Skills • EMC 5302

Name _____

The Cake

Four friends decorated this cake with gumdrops. Now they want to divide it into four pieces of equal size with the same number of gumdrops on each piece. Can you help them?

Thinking Skills • EMC 5302

You Scream! I Scream!

Introducing the Skill

1. Ask students to draw a triple-dip cone and label the flavors they would choose.

2. Share the drawings and note the different combinations of flavors. Did any student have three scoops of the same flavor? Did any student have two scoops of one flavor and one scoop of another flavor? Did any student have three different flavors?

3. Point out that each of the flavor patterns is correct and needs to be considered when determining **all** the possible ways to arrange three scoops.

Using the Chart

Use the blackline chart provided in this book or download the interactive version. (See page 3.)

1. Show Chart 9.

2. Give each student the reproduced activity page, *Three Scoops!*, on page 31. They will record possible combinations with chocolate as the first scoop.

3. If you are using the interactive chart, click on an ice-cream scoop and then choose a flavor to create new combinations.

Practicing the Skill

1. Students complete a new copy of the activity page.

2. Designate three new flavors of ice cream.

3. Have students show all the possible combinations of those three flavors.

Extending the Skill

Enjoy an ice-cream party!

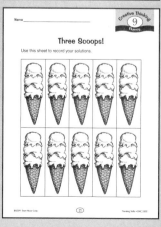

You Scream! I Scream!

How many different kinds of triple-dip cones can you make, using chocolate for the first scoop?

chocolate ICE CREAM

vanilla ICE CREAM

strawberry ICE CREAM

Thinking Skills • EMC 5302

Name _____

Three Scoops!

Use this sheet to record your solutions.

Logical Thinking

What's the Pattern?

Introducing the Skill

The skill of recognizing and using patterns is a valuable problem-solving tool. Encourage your students to describe, analyze, duplicate, and extend many different patterns.

Using the Chart

Use the blackline chart provided in this book or download the interactive version. (See page 3.)

1. Show Chart 1.

2. Read the background information below about each of the native peoples that made the blankets on the chart.

Hopi Blanket
The Hopi and the Pueblo peoples lived on top of mesas (flat-topped hills). The Hopi had homes made of rocks and mud.

The Hopi blanket has three different stripes that repeat in a pattern. The pattern is an ABCB pattern.

Arapaho Blanket
The Arapaho peoples lived on the Great Plains of the United States and traveled from place to place following herds of wild buffalo. They depended on the buffalo for almost everything they ate, wore, and used.

The Arapaho blanket has four stripes that repeat in a pattern. The pattern is an ABAC pattern if you go by color only. If you begin with white <u>and</u> use color and size of stripe, the pattern is ABCB.

Navajo Blanket
The Navajo peoples believe that the traditional patterns in their blankets simply emerge from the weavers' memories. They always leave a break within the pattern so the maker's spirit can escape.

The Navajo blanket has two stripes that repeat in a pattern. The pattern is an AB pattern.

3. Have students look carefully at one blanket at a time. The students should describe and name the patterns. If you are using the interactive chart, click on each blanket to learn more about each tribe and the pattern on their blankets.

Practicing the Skill

Students complete the activity sheet, *The Ninth Hat,* on page 35.

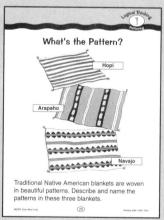

What's the Pattern?

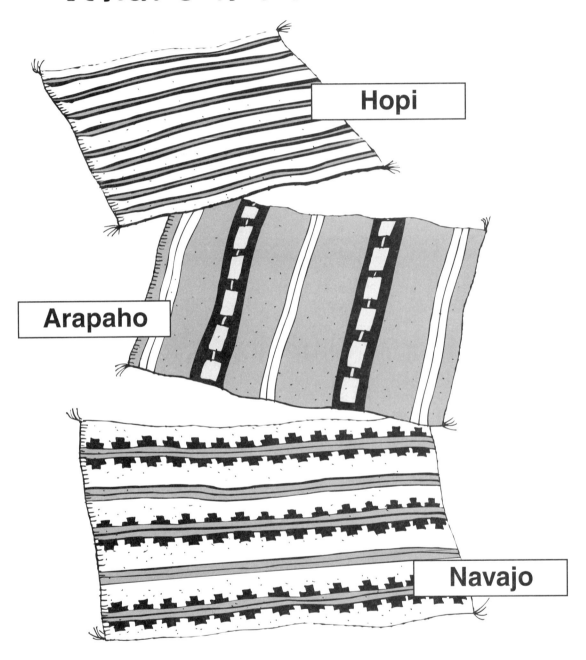

Hopi

Arapaho

Navajo

Traditional Native American blankets are woven in beautiful patterns. Describe and name the patterns in these three blankets.

The Ninth Hat

The stripes on the stocking hats are arranged in a pattern.
Figure out the pattern, and then draw the stripes on the ninth hat.

You Be Day, I'll Be Night

Introducing the Skill

Have students discuss the term **opposites**. While the term is difficult to define, students should be able to give examples to show that they understand the concept.

Using the Chart

Use the blackline chart provided in this book or download the interactive version. (See page 3.)

1. Show Chart 2.

2. Have students match the opposites illustrated on the chart.

3. Introduce **analogy** as a way to write opposites.

   • Explain that an analogy compares ideas and objects that have the same relationship. One of the relationships often used is that of opposites.

   • An analogy has a strict format: *(one thing or idea)* is to *(another thing or idea)* as *(a third thing or idea)* is to *(a fourth thing or idea)*.

      First is to **last** as **sweet** is to **sour**.

4. Write several analogies, using the sets of opposites from the chart. If you are using the interactive chart, click on the pictures to change the background color. Opposites will have the same color. Click again to change the background color back to white.

Practicing the Skill

Students complete the activity page, *You Be Day, I'll Be Night,* on page 38.

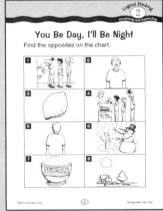

Extending the Skill

1. Divide the class into four teams.

2. Ask each team to write a word that has an antonym.

3. Have the teams pass their word to the next team, who then writes the antonym completing the first comparison.

4. Repeat two more passes to complete an analogy. For example:

   The first team writes **rich**.
   The second team might add **poor**.
   The third team writes a new word with an antonym, **city**.
   The fourth team writes **country**.

You Be Day, I'll Be Night

Find the opposites on the chart.

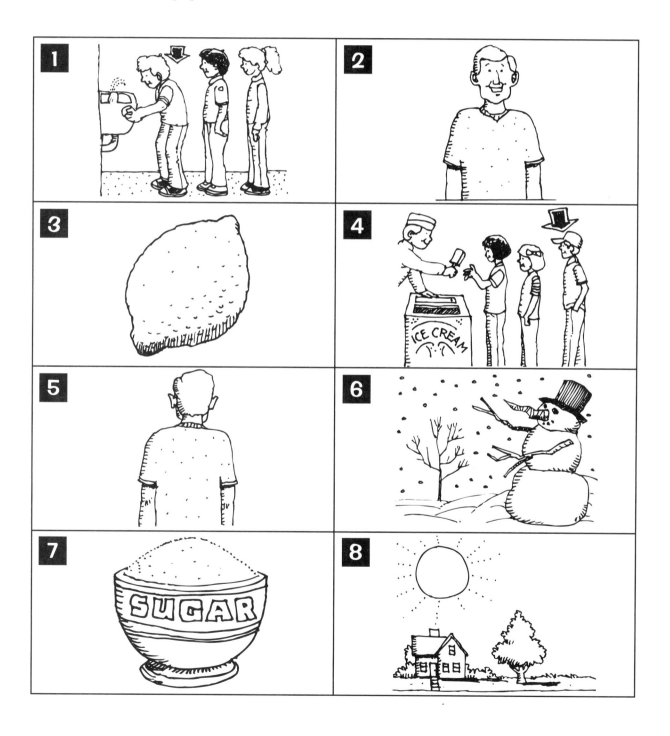

Name _____

 # You Be Day, I'll Be Night

Here are the pairs of opposite words from the chart.

> • first - last
> • sour - sweet
> • summer - winter
> • front - back

Here is a second set of opposite word pairs. On the lines below, write four analogies using one pair of words from each box.

> • fast - slow
> • hot - cold
> • early - late
> • salt - pepper

1. _____

2. _____

3. _____

4. _____

 Thinking Skills • EMC 5302

Exploring Analogies

Introducing the Skill

1. Explain that an **analogy** compares a set of objects or ideas with another set of objects or ideas. The objects or ideas may be related to each other in many different ways. For example:

   > **Bear** is to **den** as **bee** is to **hive**. *(The bear lives in the* den *and the bee lives in the* hive.)

2. Explain that many types of relationships may be used to form analogies:

numerical	*(5 : 10 :: 3 : 6)*
object-to-action	*(ear : hear :: eye : see)*
object-to-purpose	*(food : eat :: bed : sleep)*
part-to-whole	*(runner : sled :: wheel : wagon)*
sequence or degree	*(minute : small :: big : gigantic)*

Using the Chart

Use the blackline chart provided in this book or download the interactive version. (See page 3.)

1. Show Chart 3.

2. Read the incomplete analogies together.

3. Identify the relationship between the words.

4. Ask students to complete the analogies and justify their choices. If you are using the interactive chart, click on the line and keyboard the names of objects that complete the analogy correctly.

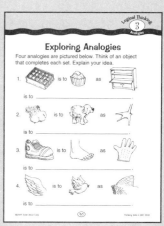

Practicing the Skill

Students complete the multiple-choice activity page, *Exploring Analogies,* on page 41.

Extending the Skill

1. Have each student write one analogy.

2. Ask students to read their analogies, leaving out the last word.

3. Have others in the class explain the relationship and give possible last words.

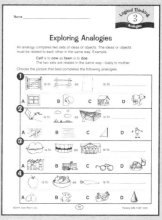

Exploring Analogies

Four analogies are pictured below. Think of an object that completes each set. Explain your idea.

1.  is to as

is to _____ .

2.  is to  as

is to _____ .

3.  is to 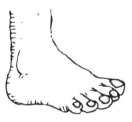 as

is to _____ .

4.  is to  as

is to _____ .

Exploring Analogies

An analogy compares two sets of ideas or objects. The ideas or objects must be related to each other in the same way. Example:

Calf is to **cow** as **fawn** is to **doe**.
The two sets are related in the same way—baby to mother.

Choose the picture that best completes the following analogies.

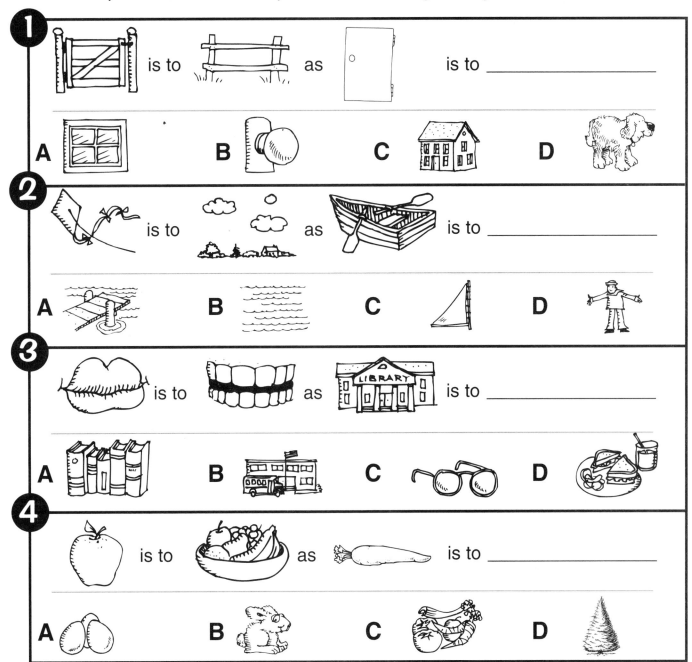

More Analogies

Introducing the Skill

1. Write several analogies on the chalkboard or overhead projector.

2. Ask students to replace the words "is to" and "as" with colons (or dots).

    is to = :   *as = ::*

3. Once the colons are in place, have students read the analogies, saying the words "is to" and "as" where there are colons.

Using the Chart

Use the blackline chart provided in this book or download the interactive version. (See page 3.)

1. Show Chart 4.

2. Have students complete each analogy and explain the relationship they referenced.

3. Have students rewrite the analogies on the chart, making new comparisons for the second half of each analogy. For example:

    bark : dog :: howl : wolf

    If you are using the interactive chart, click and drag the picture labels onto the lines to complete the analogies.

Practicing the Skill

Students complete the activity page, *More Analogies,* on page 44.

Extending the Skill

1. Divide the class into groups of four students.

2. Have each group write a list of five nouns.

3. Then ask the groups to think of a relationship for each noun and write the first half of an analogy using that relationship.

4. Have groups exchange their lists and complete each other's analogies.

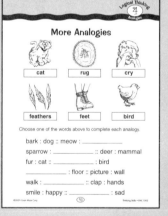

More Analogies

cat

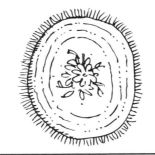

rug

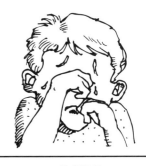

cry

feathers

feet

bird

Choose one of the words above to complete each analogy.

bark : dog :: meow : _____

sparrow : _____ :: deer : mammal

fur : cat :: _____ : bird

_____ : floor :: picture : wall

walk : _____ :: clap : hands

smile : happy :: _____ : sad

More Analogies

Dots are used to take the place of the connecting words in an analogy. Two dots are often written in place of the words "is to." Four dots mean "as."

Example: **foot** is to **leg** as **hand** is to **arm**

Can be written: foot **:** leg **::** hand **:** arm

Rewrite the following analogies using dots in place of the words.

1. **Smell** is to **nose** as **hear** is to **ear**.

_____

2. **Cub** is to **bear** as **chick** is to **hen**.

_____

3. **Air** is to **sky** as **water** is to **ocean**.

_____

Write two analogies using dots in place of the words. You may invent your own or use your favorite ones from the analogy picture chart.

_____

_____

Long Ago

Introducing the Skill

1. Show students several pictures of fish swimming in water.

2. Ask the students to make a general statement about the fish. Answers will vary, but students should infer that fish need water.

   The fish live in the water.

   The fish swim through the water.

Using the Chart

Use the blackline chart provided in this book or download the interactive version. (See page 3.)

1. Show Chart 5.

2. Have each student write a general statement about the horses on the chart. If you are using the interactive chart, click in the text box and keyboard the statement.

3. Take time to share students' statements.

Practicing the Skill

Students complete the activity page, *Pioneer Life in the 1800s,* on page 47. They will write a generalization about the story they read.

Extending the Skill

Organize a class work party for a large project to demonstrate how helping each other can be fun and productive. The project might involve making math or reading games for a class of younger students.

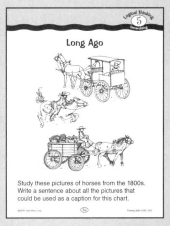

Long Ago

Study these pictures of horses from the 1800s. Write a sentence about all the pictures that could be used as a caption for this chart.

Name _____

Pioneer Life in the 1800s

Read the following story about pioneer life in the 1800s.
Write a general opinion or sentence about the way pioneers lived.

In the 1800s, pioneers moved west to find more land. Neighbors often lived miles away and couldn't visit every day. There was a lot of work to be done on farms, and people had little time for entertainment. To make life easier, pioneers had work parties. If a new barn needed to be built before winter, everyone came to help. After the work was finished, there was a large feast. Sometimes there was time after dinner for a fiddler and dancing. Women worked on quilts for the cold winters at quilting parties. Everyone helped stitch these works of art. While they worked, they could gossip and tell stories. Neighbors often helped each other harvest crops. It was a good opportunity to visit and talk with each other.

_____

_____

_____

_____

Does It Make Sense?

Introducing the Skill

Introduce the term **generalization**. Explain that generalizations are conclusions that are drawn from a set of facts. Sometimes facts can be misleading! Tell students that when making generalizations, they should consider not only the facts given, but also their own background knowledge and experiences.

Using the Chart

Use the blackline chart provided in this book or download the interactive version. (See page 3.)

1. Show Chart 6. If you are using the interactive chart, click in the text boxes to keyboard answers to the questions.

2. Have students study the illustration and list attributes for ostriches and swans. For example:

Ostriches	have feathers	have two legs
	have long necks	have beaks
Swans	have feathers	have two legs
	have long necks	have beaks

3. Ask students if swans and ostriches share attributes. Then ask if they belong to a common group because they share attributes. Have students write a generalization about ostriches and swans, naming the group.

   Ostriches and swans have feathers.
   Birds have feathers.
   So ostriches and swans are birds.

4. Have students brainstorm the attributes of giraffes.

   | **Giraffes** | have four legs | have fur |
   | | have long necks | eat leaves from trees |

5. Ask students to respond to the question on the chart about long necks.

   Ostriches and swans are birds.
   Ostriches and swans have long necks.
   So any animal with a long neck is a bird.

   Help students realize that just because an animal has a long neck doesn't mean it is a bird. Explain that the long neck generalization is not valid or true.

Practicing the Skill

Students complete the activity page, *Does It Make Sense?*, on page 50.

Does It Make Sense?

- How are an ostrich and a swan alike? How are they different?

- The animal on the right also has a long neck. Does that make it a bird?

- Why or why not?

Does It Make Sense?

Read each generalization. If it is true, write a **T** in the box. If it is not, write an **F** in the box. When you have finished, explain your answers to a partner.

☐ **1.** Barns are red buildings.
Some red buildings are houses.
So, barns are houses.

☐ **2.** Wool is a warm material.
Many coats are made of wool.
So, wool coats are warm coats.

☐ **3.** Weight lifters are energetic people.
All weight lifters are strong.
So, all energetic people are strong.

☐ **4.** Zebras are animals with stripes.
Skunks are animals with stripes.
So, skunks and zebras are related.

Read the facts below. Write a valid generalization on the lines.

5. A dime is a coin.
Coins are used as money.

So, _____

_____

6. Insects have six legs and three body parts.
A beetle is an insect.

So, _____

_____

Smith Street

Introducing the Skill

Write the word **syllogism** on the chalkboard and define it for the class:

> A syllogism is a form of reasoning that consists of two statements that are assumed to be true and a conclusion based on those statements.
>
> Sometimes the conclusion is valid or true; sometimes it is not.

Using the Chart

Use the blackline chart provided in this book or download the interactive version. (See page 3.)

1. Show Chart 7. If you are using the interactive chart, click in the text box to keyboard your response to the question "Is the syllogism still valid?"

2. Discuss the syllogism on the chart. If the first two statements are judged to be true, then the third statement, or conclusion, is valid.

3. Ask students to consider how the conclusion might change if the word "Everyone" in the first sentence was changed to "Most people." Would the conclusion still be valid? *(No, the word "most" indicates that not everyone on the street is named Smith, so Edward might be named Smith, but he wouldn't have to be named Smith.)*

4. Discuss how qualifying words, such as *all, everyone, none, few, some, often,* and *many* affect conclusions. Share the following example of an invalid conclusion:

   > *Some students in the school have a cold.*
   > *Cold germs spread quickly in schools and offices.*
   > *Therefore, all students in class will get a cold.*

   What makes this syllogism invalid? *(The word "all" in the third statement implies that everyone will get a cold.)*

   How could the third sentence be changed to make a valid conclusion? *(The qualifying words in the first and third sentences should match. If "some" is used in the first sentence, it must also be used in the conclusion—Therefore, some students in class will get a cold.)*

Practicing the Skill

Students complete the activity page, *Syllogisms,* on page 53.

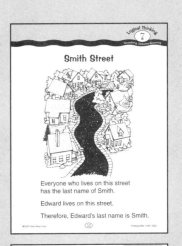

Smith Street

Everyone who lives on this street has the last name of Smith.

Edward lives on this street.

Therefore, Edward's last name is Smith.

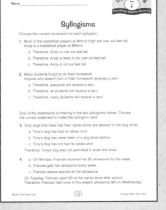

Name _____

Syllogisms

Choose the correct conclusion for each syllogism.

1. Most of the basketball players at Milford High are over six feet tall. Andy is a basketball player at Milford.
   a. Therefore, Andy is over six feet tall.
   b. Therefore, Andy is likely to be over six feet tall.
   c. Therefore, Andy is not six feet tall.

2. Many students forgot to do their homework. Anyone who doesn't turn in their homework receives a zero.
   a. Therefore, everyone will receive a zero.
   b. Therefore, all students will receive a zero.
   c. Therefore, many students will receive a zero.

One of the statements is missing in the two syllogisms below. Choose the correct statement to make the syllogism valid.

3. Only dogs that have had their rabies shots are allowed in the dog show.
   a. Tony's dog has had its rabies shot.
   b. Tony's dog has never been in a dog show before.
   c. Tony's dog has not had its rabies shot.
   Therefore, Tony's dog was not permitted to enter the show.

4. a. On Monday, Frances received her $5 allowance for the week.
   b. Frances gets her allowance every week.
   c. Frances always spends all her allowance.
   On Tuesday, Frances spent $5 at the candy store after school. Therefore, Frances had none of this week's allowance left on Wednesday.

Smith Street

Everyone who lives on this street has the last name of Smith.

Edward lives on this street.

Therefore, Edward's last name is Smith.

Syllogisms

Choose the correct conclusion for each syllogism.

1. Most of the basketball players at Milford High are over six feet tall.
    Andy is a basketball player at Milford.

    a. Therefore, Andy is over six feet tall.

    b. Therefore, Andy is likely to be over six feet tall.

    c. Therefore, Andy is not six feet tall.

2. Many students forgot to do their homework.
    Anyone who doesn't turn in their homework receives a zero.

    a. Therefore, everyone will receive a zero.

    b. Therefore, all students will receive a zero.

    c. Therefore, many students will receive a zero.

One of the statements is missing in the two syllogisms below. Choose
the correct statement to make the syllogism valid.

3. Only dogs that have had their rabies shots are allowed in the dog show.

    a. Tony's dog has had its rabies shot.

    b. Tony's dog has never been in a dog show before.

    c. Tony's dog has not had its rabies shot.

    Therefore, Tony's dog was not permitted to enter the show.

4. a. On Monday, Frances received her $5 allowance for the week.

    b. Frances gets her allowance every week.

    c. Frances always spends all her allowance.

    On Tuesday, Frances spent $5 at the candy store after school.
    Therefore, Frances had none of this week's allowance left on Wednesday.

Silly Syllogisms

Introducing the Skill

1. Review and post the syllogism rules.

2. Remind students that a correctly written syllogism is not necessarily true. The first two sentences don't have to be valid, but they must support the third.

Using the Chart

Use the blackline chart provided in this book or download the interactive version. (See page 3.)

1. Show Chart 8. If you are using the interactive chart, click on each picture to change it to a word.

2. Read the syllogisms together.

3. Have students copy the syllogisms and determine whether they are valid.

Practicing the Skill

Students complete the activity page, *More Syllogisms,* on page 56.

Extending the Skill

1. Have students choose a product. For example: *Space Bars*

2. Have students write a syllogism about the product. For example:

> *All famous people eat Space Bars.*
>
> *Some baseball players are famous.*
>
> *Therefore, some baseball players eat Space Bars.*

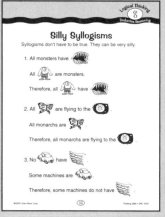

Silly Syllogisms

Syllogisms don't have to be true. They can be very silly.

1. All monsters have .

   All are monsters.

   Therefore, all have .

2. All 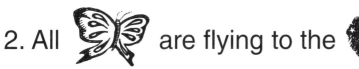 are flying to the .

   All monarchs are .

   Therefore, all monarchs are flying to the .

3. No have .

   Some machines are .

   Therefore, some machines do not have .

 Thinking Skills • EMC 5302

More Syllogisms

Sometimes syllogisms are invalid. That means the first two ideas don't prove the third part of the syllogism. Example:

All books have pages.
All magazines have pages.
Therefore, all magazines are books.

Even though both books and magazines have pages, they are <u>not</u> the same. It is almost the same as saying tigers and zebras both have stripes; therefore, they are the same animal. These syllogisms are invalid.

Make an **X** in front of the syllogisms that are invalid.

1. _____   All candy is sweet.
Some cereals are sweet.
Therefore, some cereals are candy.

2. _____   All plants are green.
All grasses are plants.
Therefore, all grasses are green.

3. _____   The moon is made of green cheese.
Green cheese is covered with mold.
Therefore, the moon is covered with mold.

4. _____   All Martians are blue.
All violets are blue.
Therefore, all violets are Martians.

Who Ate the Cookies in the Cookie Jar?

Introducing the Skill

1. Copy this matrix (without answers) onto the chalkboard or use the interactive chart. If you are using the interactive chart, drag an **X** or a **yes** into each box.

	Chocolate Chip	Peanut Butter
Zeke	2 X	2 X
Esther	5 X	5 X
Anita	6 X	6 X
Alice	1 X	7 X
Sara	Yes	3 X
Spot	X	Yes

2. Explain to the class that a matrix provides a method of recording the information given so that you arrive at correct answers through a process of eliminating incorrect answers. Sometimes you must read through all the clues a number of times before marking any spaces on the matrix.

Using the Chart

Use the blackline chart provided in this book or download the interactive version. (See page 3.)

1. Show Chart 9.

2. Guide students as they read the clues. Show them how to mark the matrix as each piece of information is evaluated. The small numbers on the sample matrix show which clues provide the information needed to make the *X* or write *yes*.

Practicing the Skill

If your class has no previous experience with logic matrixes, you may wish to begin the student page together.

Students complete the activity page, *Whose Soup?,* on page 59.

Extending the Skill

1. Challenge students to make their own logic puzzles matching five students and five games they like to play.

2. To begin, have students match the games and the students on an answer sheet.

3. Then have students write clues that will help others solve the puzzles.

Who Ate the Cookies in the Cookie Jar?

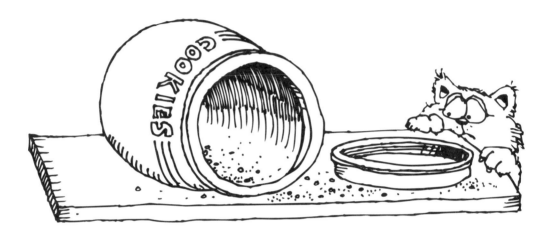

Sometime between noon and 3 o'clock, four chocolate chip cookies and one peanut butter cookie disappeared from the cookie jar. Who ate the cookies?

1. Alice doesn't like chocolate.

2. Zeke worked in the garden with Aunt Sally all afternoon.

3. Sara doesn't like peanut butter cookies.

4. Esther and Anita like chocolate chip and peanut butter cookies.

5. Esther can't reach the cookie jar.

6. Esther said Anita didn't eat any cookies.

7. Peanut butter gives Alice an itchy rash.

8. Esther and Anita played together in the garden all afternoon.

9. Sara said she saw Spot eating a cookie that was on the floor.

Thinking Skills • EMC 5302

Name _____

Whose Soup?

Fill in the information on the matrix.

When you know that a soup is **not** someone's favorite, make an **X** in that box.

When you know that a soup **is** someone's favorite, write **yes** in that box.

	tomato soup	vegetable soup	chicken noodle soup	bean soup
Edward				
Lisa				
Ben				
Lara				

• Edward doesn't like chicken noodle soup.

• Lisa makes her own soup with carrots and peas from her garden.

• Lara doesn't like bean or chicken noodle soup.

• Ben has never tasted soup that begins with the first letter of his name.

Where Is Burton?

Introducing the Skill

Working with matrix and table logic puzzles helps students organize their thinking. If your students have no previous experience with either logic puzzle, you will want to work through the puzzles together. Encourage the students to discuss their reasoning.

Using the Chart

Use the blackline chart provided in this book or download the interactive version. (See page 3.)

1. Show Chart 10.

2. Have students draw a table with eight chairs. Note that the chair on one end of the table is turned upside down, so no one can sit on it.

3. Read each clue and label the chairs as you learn information about the location of each student. If you are using the interactive chart, click on each chair to keyboard the name of the student occupying the chair.

Practicing the Skill

1. Give students the activity page, *New Signs on Main Street*, on page 62.

2. Explain that the top part of the activity page shows a map of Main Street. The middle part of the page lists the store names in a matrix.

3. Read the clues given at the bottom of the page. Evaluate the information in each clue together, and then record the information by making *Xs* or writing *yes* on the grid.

Where Is Burton?

It's the first day of kindergarten.
Follow the clues and help Ms. Martinez find Burton.

- Maria is seated between her friends, Ali and Omar.

- Carla is at the end of the table.

- Omar is seated next to the empty chair.

- Ali is seated near Carla's left hand.

- Alex is next to the empty chair.

- Ana is seated on the left side of Alex.

Where is Burton seated?

 Thinking Skills • EMC 5302

New Signs on Main Street

Use the clues and the matrix to solve the following puzzle.

There are eight stores on Main Street. The store owners took down their signs and asked Mr. Baldwin to paint new ones. Mr. Baldwin decided to put the new signs up at night after the stores were closed. Help Mr. Baldwin match the signs and the stores.

Park	A	B	C	D

Main Street

E	F	G	H	Parking Lot

Signs	A	B	C	D	E	F	G	H
Shoe Tree								
Young's Yummy Yogurt								
Delicious Deli								
Star Theater								
Fancy Duds								
Fix-It Hardware								
Food! Food!								
Animal Barn								

- There is one building between Fancy Duds and the parking lot.
- The deli and the yogurt shop are next to each other.
- The deli is next to Fancy Duds.
- The grocery store is between the shoe store and the hardware store.
- The hardware store is next to the park.
- The movie theater is next to the parking lot.

Let's Go Ice-Skating

Introducing the Skill

1. Draw a simple version of this map on the board to share with the class.

2. Ask students to explain how to travel from one place to another.

3. Students might work in pairs for more practice. For example, one person can explain how to move from point A to point C, and the other from point A to point R.

Using the Chart

Use the blackline chart provided in this book or download the interactive version. (See page 3.)

1. Show Chart 11.

2. Have students suggest several routes.

3. If you are using the interactive chart, click in the text box to keyboard the directions. Students may also write their own version of the best route.

Practicing the Skill

Students complete the activity page, *From Here to There,* on page 65.

Extending the Skill

Ask students to bring in different types of maps, including ones of oceans, weather, roads, and landforms. Display the maps and discuss what can be learned from each kind of map.

Let's Go Ice-Skating

Samantha and Bernie are going ice-skating at the Ice Palace.
Bernie needs directions. What directions will Samantha give
to Bernie about how to get to the Ice Palace?

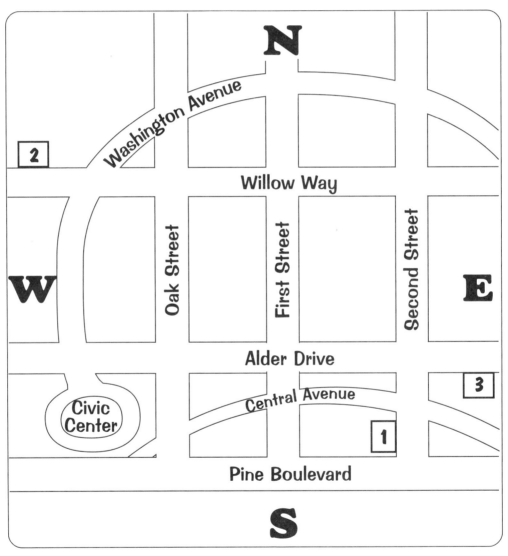

KEY
1. Ice Palace
2. Bernie's House
3. Samantha's House

Thinking Skills • EMC 5302

Name _____

From Here to There

Draw a map showing your house and a store. Write the directions for getting from the house to the store.

Read the directions to a classmate. Have him or her follow the directions to draw a map. Compare the two maps. Are they the same or different?

_____

_____

_____

_____

_____

Thinking Skills • EMC 5302

Backyard Projects

Introducing the Skill

Explain to students that solving logic problems using a chart or simple map follows many of the same thought processes that matrix problems require.

- Students are asked to figure out how two or more sets of facts relate to each other *(for example, who lives in which house).*

- All the facts that students will need to solve the puzzle are given.

- As students eliminate possibilities, they will narrow down the choices until they can establish a certainty. That certainty will usually help narrow down the possibilities in another set of facts.

Using the Chart

Use the blackline chart provided in this book or download the interactive version. (See page 3.)

1. Show Chart 12.

2. Read one clue at a time. Make notes on the chart to help synthesize information.

   If you are using the interactive chart, you are provided with a matrix chart to help you solve the problem. Click on the picture to see the first clue. Click on the list of clues to see additional clues. Drag an *X* or a *yes* into each spot on the matrix.

3. Here are the clues for solving the puzzle:

   a. *Three young people—Ivan, the person who is making a fishpond, and the person who is building a fort—live on the same side of the street. The other two, Maurice and the person who is hanging a new tire swing, live on the other side.*

   b. *Tom's house number is higher than Carmen's, whose number is higher than that of the friend who is building a skateboard jump.*

   c. *Breanne and the person working on a giant sandbox live on the same side of the street but are not immediate neighbors.*

   d. *Carmen is not building a sandbox. She is the next-door neighbor of the fort builder, whose address is the highest.*

Practicing the Skill

Students complete the activity page, *Four Treehouses*, on page 68.

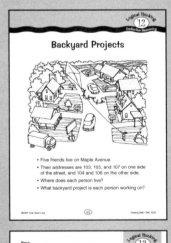

Backyard Projects

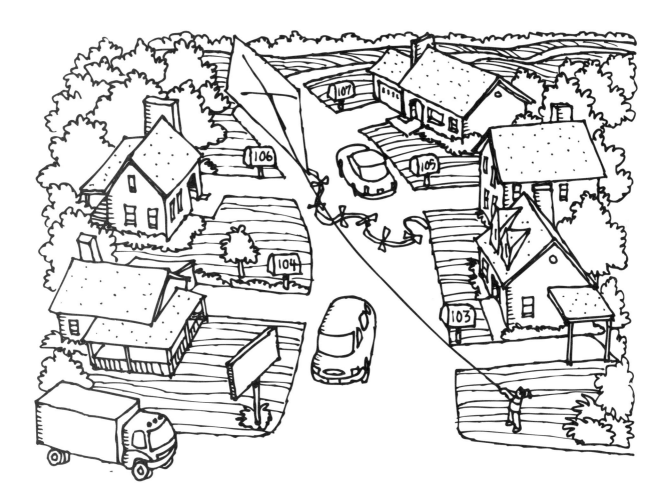

- Five friends live on Maple Avenue.

- Their addresses are 103, 105, and 107 on one side of the street, and 104 and 106 on the other side.

- Where does each person live?

- What backyard project is each person working on?

Four Treehouses

Jose and three of his friends—Sabrina, Alex, and Nga—live in the four houses on the north side of Fifth Street. Each of the friends has a treehouse. All of the treehouses are different.

Read the clues below. Figure out which treehouse belongs to each person. Label each treehouse with its owner's name.

1. Sabrina's next-door neighbor has a two-story treehouse.

2. Alex does **not** have a ladder in his treehouse.

3. The treehouse on the west side of Sabrina's belongs to Nga.

At the Amusement Park

Introducing the Skill

Review the process for solving matrix logic puzzles. Say:

To do matrix logic problems, start by gathering information from the clues. Use the matrix (grid) to keep track of the facts that you gather. Mark the boxes with **X** *for* **no** *or* **yes** *in the correct answer box. Only one box in each row and column can have a* **yes**.

Using the Chart

Use the blackline chart provided in this book or download the interactive version. (See page 3.)

1. Show Chart 13.

2. Read the situation below.

   Hernaldo took five friends, Alicia, Ann, Rachel, Raul, and Tim, to the amusement park. Each one rode a different ride first. Read the clues and find out who rode which ride first.

3. With your students, read each clue and solve the puzzle. If you are using the interactive chart, drag an *X* or a *yes* to each square in the grid to solve the puzzle.

Practicing the Skill

Students complete the activity page, *Which Pet?*, on page 71.

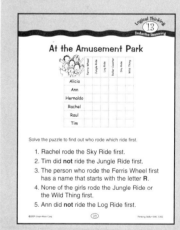

At the Amusement Park

	Ferris Wheel	Jungle Ride	Log Ride	Roller Coaster	Sky Ride	Wild Thing
Alicia						
Ann						
Hernaldo						
Rachel						
Raul						
Tim						

Solve the puzzle to find out who rode which ride first.

1. Rachel rode the Sky Ride first.

2. Tim did **not** ride the Jungle Ride first.

3. The person who rode the Ferris Wheel first has a name that starts with the letter **R**.

4. None of the girls rode the Jungle Ride or the Wild Thing first.

5. Ann did **not** ride the Log Ride first.

Thinking Skills • EMC 5302

Which Pet?

Solve the puzzle to find out which pet belongs to each child. Make an **X** in a box if a person does **not** own a certain pet. Write **yes** in the box when you know which pet a person owns.

	Tom	Rascal	Smiley	Dipsey	Curly	Fido
Arlene						
Carlos						
Cecelia						
Chad						
Juan						
Nancy						

- Curly and its owner do **not** have names that begin with the same letter.

- Either Nancy or Cecelia own the fish.

- The boy who owns the cat, Smiley's owner, and Chad live on the same street.

- Arlene owns the turtle.

- Juan owns either the rabbit or the snake.

- Cecelia loves her pet Dipsey.

What's Next?

Introducing the Skill

Finding patterns in a sequence requires students to discover how numbers are related. Once the relationship is uncovered, the next step in the sequence can be predicted.

Using the Chart

Use the blackline chart provided in this book or download the interactive version. (See page 3.)

1. Show Chart 14.

2. Have students analyze the five numbers given and find a relationship between them. If students cannot see a relationship, ask, *Is the first number larger or smaller than the second? How much larger or smaller? Is the third number larger or smaller than the second? How much larger or smaller?*

3. Then have students suggest the next four numbers in the sequence. If you are using the interactive chart, click on the question mark in the clouds without numbers and keyboard the correct number to continue the sequence.

Practicing the Skill

Students complete the activity page, *Can You Find the Number Pattern?,* on page 74.

Extending the Skill

Determining number patterns is helpful when solving math problems. Share the following math word problem with your students. Then demonstrate how the number pattern below provides the answer to the problem.

> The students in Mrs. Butterworth's class wanted to make a quilt for their art project.
>
> • First, they made 28 small quilt squares.
>
> • Then they sewed the small squares together to make the quilt.
>
> It took 12 minutes to sew 4 of the small squares together into one larger square. How long did it take them to sew **all** the small squares into larger squares?

Squares used:	4	8	12	16	20	24	28
Time in minutes:	12	24	36	48	60	72	84

What's Next?

Think about the pattern. What are the next four numbers in this sequence?

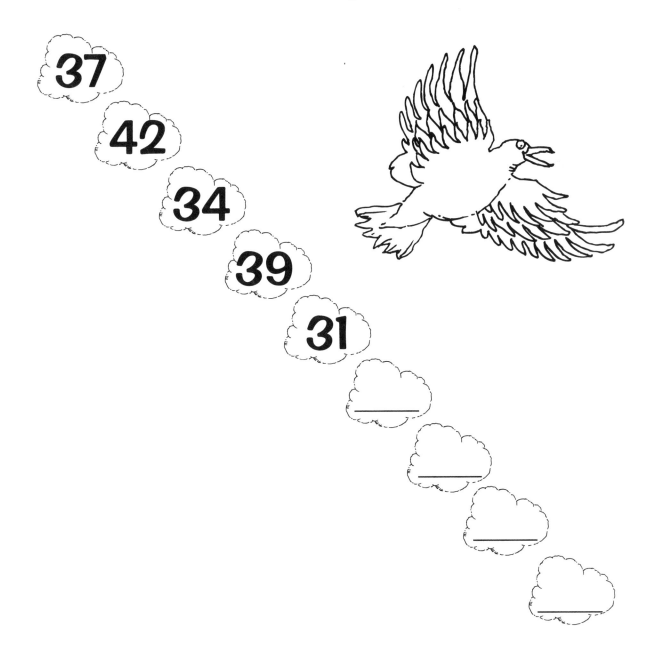

37

42

34

39

31

_____

_____

_____

_____

Can You Find the Number Pattern?

Think about each number sequence below. Determine the pattern and then predict the next numbers in the sequence. Write what the pattern is on the line.

A 45, 36, 28, 21, _____, _____, _____

_____

B 2, 1, 3, 2, 4, _____, _____, _____

_____

C 4, 9, 16, 25, _____, _____

_____

D 103, 204, 305, _____, _____

_____

E 132, 243, 354, 465, _____, _____

_____

Off to Camp!

Introducing the Skill

1. Remind students that solving logic puzzles requires them to think carefully about the clues that they are given.

2. Have students cut out the campers on the reproducible page so that they can manipulate them as you read the clues.

3. Each student should have five cards or pieces of paper to represent the five bunks. Each card should be folded in half and labeled *top* and *bottom*.

Using the Chart

Use the blackline chart provided in this book or download the interactive version. (See page 3.)

1. Show Chart 15.

2. Write the following clues on a transparency or chart. If you are using the interactive chart, click on and drag the campers' names to the beds as you read the clues.

   a. *Fred, Ted, and Ed (the triplets) do <u>not</u> want to sleep in the same bunk.*

   b. *Ben, Fred, Pete, and Igor want top bunks.*

   c. *Ted, Franz, and Ed want bottom bunks.*

   d. *Hernando and Franz need to be able to see out a window while lying in bed.*

   e. *Ed and Hernando want to share a bunk, as do Nate and Fred.*

   f. *Sam and Igor want to be bunkmates.*

   g. *Both Sam and Pete like being in an end bunk.*

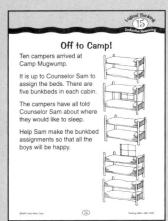

Practicing the Skill

1. Have students use the camper cutouts on page 77 to create a new puzzle.

2. Reread the clues for Chart 15 before asking students to write the clues for the new puzzle. Point out that the clues tell relationships among the boys, but do not give exact locations.

3. Assign the following task:

   Divide the ten boys into two equal teams, and then write clues that will help others identify the teams that the boys are on.

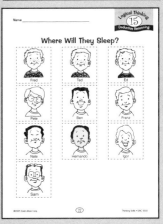

Off to Camp!

Ten campers arrived at Camp Mugwump.

It is up to Counselor Sam to assign the beds. There are five bunkbeds in each cabin.

The campers have all told Counselor Sam about where they would like to sleep.

Help Sam make the bunkbed assignments so that all the boys will be happy.

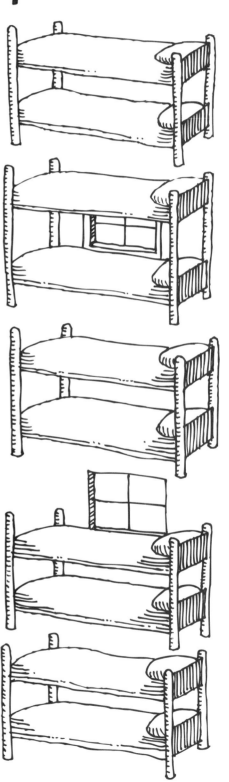

Where Will They Sleep?

Fred	Ted	Ed
Pete	Ben	Franz
Nate	Hernando	Igor
Sam		

Look Again!

Introducing the Skill

1. Draw a large right triangle on the chalkboard. Ask students how many triangles they see. *(one)*

2. Draw a line that divides the triangle into two triangles. Ask students again. *(Some students may say two. Remind them that there are two small triangles plus the original large triangle. So there are three.)*

3. Remind students that when they analyze a figure, they must identify and focus on **all** of the parts. They may focus, at first, on the shapes of only one size or type. Direct students to look for shapes of different sizes and different shapes.

Using the Chart

Use the blackline chart provided in this book or download the interactive version. (See page 3.)

1. Show Chart 16.

2. Trace each triangle, using a different color pen or a different type of line.

3. Count the triangles. If you are using the interactive chart, click on the triangle to show a progression of triangles that will help students identify the total number on the chart.

Practicing the Skill

Students complete the activity page, *Triangle Mania,* on page 80.

Extending the Skill

Use pattern blocks to create large shapes. Challenge students to count the component shapes.

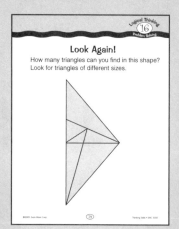

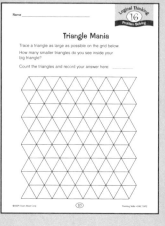

Look Again!

How many triangles can you find in this shape?
Look for triangles of different sizes.

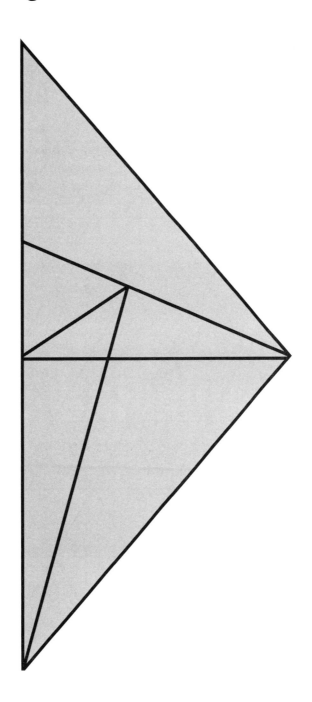

Thinking Skills • EMC 5302

Triangle Mania

Trace a triangle as large as possible on the grid below.

How many smaller triangles do you see inside your big triangle?

Count the triangles and record your answer here: _____

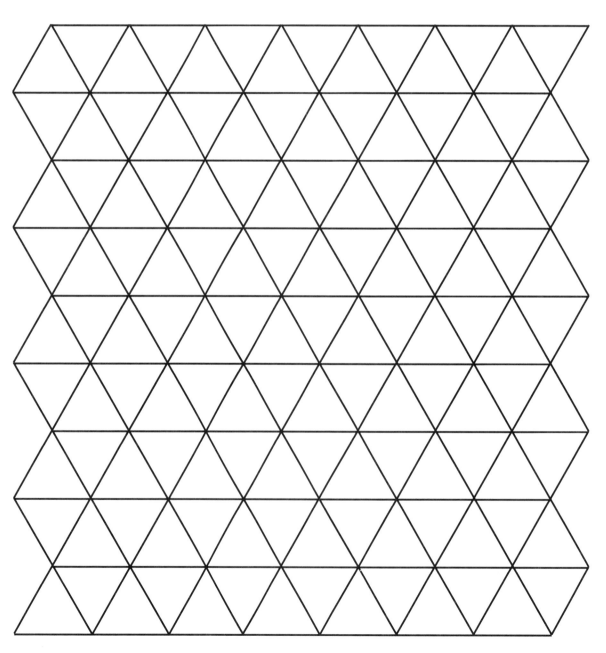

Critical Thinking

Curly Q's

Introducing the Skill

Discuss the term **attributes** with your class. Say:

An attribute is a particular characteristic of an object or a living thing. For example, you can say books have covers and pages. The cover and the pages are attributes of a book. So a dictionary, a comic book, and a spiral notebook are all books because they have covers and pages.

Using the Chart

Use the blackline chart provided in this book or download the interactive version. (See page 3.)

1. Show Chart 1. The chart requires students to identify the common attributes of a set of imaginary creatures called Curly Q's.

2. Have students look closely at the three Curly Q's in the first row. Ask, *What attributes do they have in common?* (They each have a circle face, two eyes, one curlicue, no facial features other than the eyes, and a body.)

3. Have students look at the three figures that are not Curly Q's. Ask, *How are these figures different from the Curly Q's in the first row?* (One has a frown, one has two curlicues, and one has a square face.)

4. Finally, have students study the third row of figures. Ask, *Which figures have all the attributes of the Curly Q's in the first row?* (Only the first one is a Curly Q. The second has a smile. The third has no curlicue.)

   If you are using the interactive chart, click on the figures in the far right column to see if they fit the category of Curly Q's.

Practicing the Skill

Students complete the activity page, *Cool Dogs,* on page 84.

Extending the Skill

1. Ask students to draw another imaginary figure that could be a Curly Q.

2. Share the drawings and check to see that each new Curly Q has the attributes necessary to earn its title.

Curly Q's

These are Curly Q's:

These are **not** Curly Q's:

Are these Curly Q's?

Thinking Skills • EMC 5302

Name _____

Cool Dogs

These are Cool Dogs:

These are **not** Cool Dogs:

Draw a Cool Dog here:

What are the attributes of a Cool Dog?

1. _____

2. _____

3. _____

Thinking Skills • EMC 5302

The Cat Family

Introducing the Skill

Explain to your students that real objects and living things both have attributes. This activity requires that students use their prior knowledge and research skills to identify common attributes in cats.

Using the Chart

Use the blackline chart provided in this book or download the interactive version. (See page 3.)

1. Show Chart 2.

2. Have students list common attributes of cats. Record the attributes.

   If you are using the interactive chart, click in the text box to keyboard students' responses.

3. Provide reference materials for students to read and discover more facts about cats.

4. Add any new information found to the list. For example:

   Some Common Attributes of Cats

   • *A pair of teeth on each side of the jaw form large cross-shearing blades for cutting meat.*

   • *The tongue is covered with sharp, curved projections used for rasping meat off bones, cleaning the fur, and drinking.*

   • *Cats have five toes on each front foot and four toes on each hind foot. The fifth digit is positioned high on each hind leg.*

   • *The claws can be retracted.*

Practicing the Skill

Students complete the activity page, *How Are They Alike?,* on page 87. This activity requires the use of inference as well as prior knowledge. For example, gears are visible on a bicycle; many students will know that motorized vehicles have gears as well.

Extending the Skill

Have students write a summary paragraph stating the common attributes of the cat family.

The Cat Family

What characteristics do **all** the members of the cat family share?

Thinking Skills • EMC 5302

How Are They Alike?

List the attributes that these vehicles have in common.

_____

_____

_____

_____

_____

_____

The Animal Club

Introducing the Skill

Guide your students through the process of discovering a single
animal that has attributes unique to a particular group.

Using the Chart

Use the blackline chart provided in this book or download the
interactive version. (See page 3.)

1. Show Chart 3.

2. Have students identify the common attributes of **all** the animals
   on the chart. (They all are living things, they have tails, they hunt
   for food, etc.) Record students' responses.

   If you are using the interactive chart, click in the text box to
   keyboard students' responses.

3. Ask, *Are there attributes that are different for two or more of the
   animals?* (Some live on land and others in the water, some are
   warmblooded and others are coldblooded, etc.) Record students'
   responses.

4. Ask, *Is there one attribute that only one animal does not have?*
   (They all have four feet and breathe with lungs except for one.)
   Record students' responses.

5. Conclude that membership to the Animal Club must depend on
   two shared attributes: having four feet and breathing with lungs.
   Therefore, the animal that is different from all the rest is the fish.

Practicing the Skill

1. Students complete the activity page, *It's Not in the Club,*
   on page 90.

2. Share the information with the class. Make sure that students can
   articulate the reason why each item does not belong with the
   others in the line.

Extending the Skill

Have students compare people by listing their attributes. Have them
look for leadership characteristics when comparing historical figures,
such as Abraham Lincoln and George Washington.

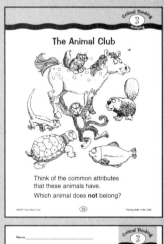

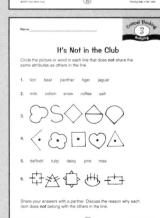

The Animal Club

Think of the common attributes that these animals have.

Which animal does **not** belong?

Thinking Skills • EMC 5302

Name _____

It's Not in the Club

Circle the picture or word in each line that does **not** share the same attributes as others in the line.

1.　lion　　bear　　panther　　tiger　　jaguar

2.　milk　　cotton　　snow　　coffee　　salt

3.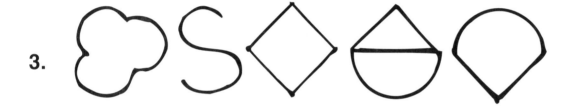

4.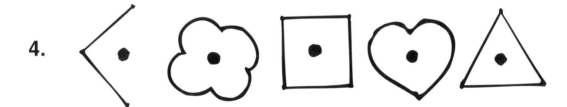

5.　daffodil　　tulip　　daisy　　pine　　rose

6.

Share your answers with a partner. Discuss the reason why each item does **not** belong with the others in the line.

　　　　90　　　　Thinking Skills • EMC 5302

What Doesn't Belong?

Introducing the Skill

Classifying involves comparing and contrasting specific items, and then arranging them together in categories.

Using the Chart

Use the blackline chart provided in this book or download the interactive version. (See page 3.)

1. Show Chart 4.

2. Have students name each picture on the page. *(firecracker, wreath, turkey, car, heart, shamrock, jack-o'-lantern)*

3. Ask students to identify the one picture on the page that might not belong with the others. *(car)*

4. Have students tell how **all** the other pictures are alike. *(They are related to American holidays.)*

5. Ask students to suggest a title that tells about **all** the pictures on the page except the car. *(holiday symbols)*

   If you are using the interactive chart, click in the text box to keyboard students' responses.

Practicing the Skill

Students complete the activity page, *What Doesn't Belong?*, on page 93.

Extending the Skill

1. Make a set of 20 index cards, labeling each one with the name of a different general category (for example, *fruit, boys' names, clothing, TV shows, book titles, countries, states, etc.*).

2. On the back of each card, list five items that belong in the category named on the front.

3. Provide a 3-minute timer and a coin to use with this game.

4. Form two teams of two or three players each. Ask for a volunteer to be the game moderator.

5. Flip the coin to see which team starts first. Have the moderator draw a category card and read aloud the category. The team has 3 minutes to call out as many items as they can that belong in that category. Every time they name an item listed on the backside of the card, they score one point. After time is up, the second team chooses a different category. Give each team a chance to use 10 cards. The team with the most points is the winner.

What Doesn't Belong?

Which picture on this page does **not** belong?

Why doesn't it belong?

How would you classify **all** the remaining pictures on this page?

Critical Thinking
4
Analyzing, Classifying

What Doesn't Belong?

Draw a line through the one word in each line that does **not** belong.
Circle the one word in each line that tells about all the other words.

1. clown   lion   tent   circus   easel   horse

2. farm   barn   bus   silo   horse   wagon

3. multiplication   addition   capitalization   subtraction   mathematics   division

4. running   galloping   prancing   moving   jumping   neighing

5. heart   organs   kidneys   arms   stomach   lungs

On the blank line, write a word or words that tell about **all** the words in the line.

6. Lincoln   Washington   Reagan   Roosevelt   Kennedy   Jefferson   Bush

_____

7. stop   slow   yield   caution   go   cross _____

8. milk   cheese   sour cream   yogurt   ice cream _____

Write three words that would fit into each category named below.

9. chewy foods: _____   _____   _____

10. ballgames: _____   _____   _____

Connections

Introducing the Skill

1. Write the following words on the chalkboard:

   peas, carrots, lettuce, pears

   minutes, clock, hours, seconds

2. Explain that one word in each set does not belong. Ask students to name the word that doesn't belong.

3. Have students explain the attribute the other three words share.

Using the Chart

Use the blackline chart provided in this book or download the interactive version. (See page 3.)

1. Show Chart 5.

2. Have students name the pictures in a row.

3. They should identify the one picture that doesn't belong and tell how the other three pictures are related. If you are using the interactive chart, drag an *X* onto each of the pictures that don't belong in their row.

Practicing the Skill

Students complete the activity page, *Connections,* on page 96.

Extending the Skill

1. Have students list 10 subjects (for example, *Things That Fly*).

2. Then ask students to list as many nouns as they can that fit under each subject. Record students' answers on a chart.

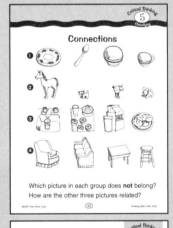

Connections

Which picture in each group does **not** belong?
How are the other three pictures related?

Name _____

Connections

Three of the words in each of the groups below have a special relationship. On the lines, write an explanation of how they are alike. Then circle the word that does **not** belong.

1. pencil   pen   paintbrush   paper

_____

2. book   magazine   TV   newspaper

_____

3. broom   furniture polish   mop   vacuum

_____

4. circle   triangle   square   rectangle

_____

5. shirt   jeans   shoes   underwear

_____

6. floor   ceiling   wall   roof

_____

7. river   lake   stream   brook

_____

Thinking Skills • EMC 5302

A Sizable Matter

Introducing the Skill

Explain that the sizes of students in the classroom vary. Not all boys are the same height and weight. Not all girls are the same height and weight. The sizes of animals vary too. The sizes given on the chart are averages (i.e., some aardvarks <u>don't</u> weigh 150 pounds) and may be used to classify the animals.

Using the Chart

Use the blackline chart provided in this book or download the interactive version. (See page 3.)

1. Show Chart 6.

2. Have students list the animals from the largest to the smallest.

3. Hopefully, a student will ask whether the size you are referring to is the height to the shoulder, the weight, or the length. If this question doesn't come up, ask students if there is more than one way to compare the size of the animals.

4. List the animals using the three different size comparisons.

   If you are using the interactive chart, click in the text box to keyboard a list of the animal names.

Practicing the Skill

1. Give each student a copy of the activity page, *A Sizable Matter,* on page 99.

2. Explain that students are to read more about each mammal and then identify a variety of attributes that could be used to group the mammals (for example, *Hairy and Little Hair*).

3. Have students list the attributes on a separate sheet of paper and then group the animals in each different classification. Explain that if there isn't enough information given to include an animal in one of the groups, it should be labeled "unclassified."

Extending the Skill

Have students add the names of five of their favorite animals to those listed on the student page. Drawing on their prior knowledge, have students add these names to the appropriate classification lists.

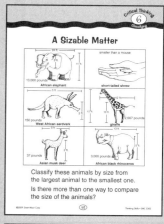

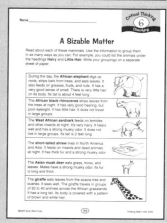

A Sizable Matter

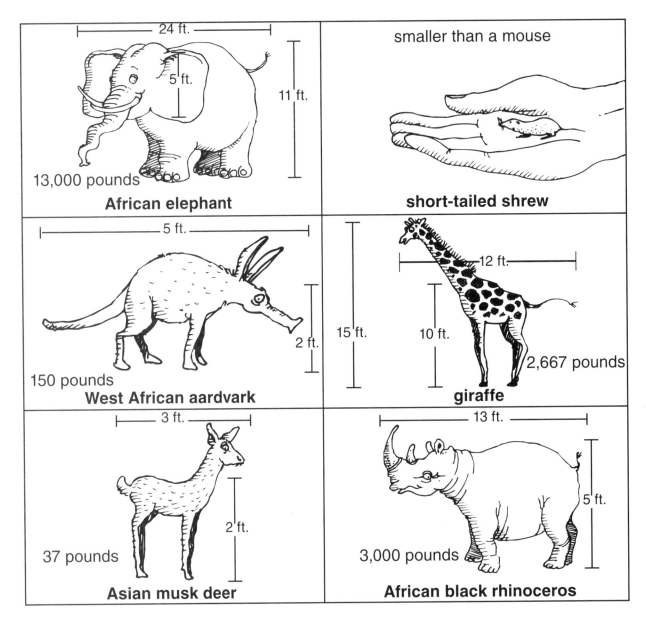

24 ft.	smaller than a mouse
5 ft. 11 ft.	
13,000 pounds	
African elephant	**short-tailed shrew**

5 ft.

2 ft.

150 pounds

West African aardvark

12 ft.

15 ft. 10 ft.

2,667 pounds

giraffe

3 ft.

2 ft.

37 pounds

Asian musk deer

13 ft.

5 ft.

3,000 pounds

African black rhinoceros

Classify these animals by size from
the largest animal to the smallest one.

Is there more than one way to compare
the size of the animals?

Thinking Skills • EMC 5302

Name _____

A Sizable Matter

Read about each of these mammals. Use the information to group them in as many ways as you can. For example, you could list the animals under the headings **Hairy** and **Little Hair**. Write your groupings on a separate sheet of paper.

During the day, the **African elephant** digs up roots, strips bark from trees, and eats leaves. It also feeds on grasses, fruits, and nuts. It has a very good sense of smell. There is very little hair on its body. Its tail is about 4 feet long.	
The **African black rhinoceros** strips leaves from the trees at night. It has very good hearing, but poor eyesight. It has little hair. It does not travel in large groups.	
The **West African aardvark** feeds on termites and other insects at night. It's very hairy. It hears well and has a strong musky odor. It does not live in large groups. Its tail is 2 feet long.	
The **short-tailed shrew** lives in North America and Asia. It feeds on insects and dead animals at night. It has thick fur and a strong musky odor.	
The **Asian musk deer** eats grass, moss, and leaves. Males have a strong musky odor. Its fur is long and thick.	
The **giraffe** eats leaves from the acacia tree and bushes. It sees well. The giraffe travels in groups of 20 to 40 animals across the African grasslands. It has a long tail. Its body is covered with a pattern of brown and white hair.	

The Most Important Things

Introducing the Skill

1. Ask students to think about what they would do in the following situation:

   It's snack time. You open your lunchbox to find that your mother packed an apple for your snack. A friend offers you a delicious candy bar in exchange for the apple. Do you eat the healthy snack your mother intended for you, or do you swap it for the candy bar that you know is not very healthy, but that you want anyway?

2. Have students write their choices on a piece of paper. In this way, each student is committed to a choice. Then ask volunteers to give reasons for their choices.

Using the Chart

Use the blackline chart provided in this book or download the interactive version. (See page 3.)

1. Show Chart 7.

2. Explain that to **prioritize** means to rank items according to their importance to each individual, based on that person's values, interests, and likes. Probably no two people will prioritize in the very same way.

3. Ask students to prioritize the items on the chart. If you are using the interactive chart, click and drag the items beside a number to prioritize them.

   Note: If some students have difficulty ranking the list, break the activity down into smaller choices. For example, ask students if they would rather have a nice house or cool clothes. Would they rather get good grades or have a lot of toys?

4. After students complete the activity, divide the class into small groups of three to five. Ask students to share their rankings with the group and to explain why they prioritized as they did.

5. Discuss the drawbacks of making priority rankings. (Everyone's ranking may be different; priorities might change depending on the time the choices were made.)

Practicing the Skill

Students complete the activity page, *The Most Important Things*, on page 102.

The Most Important Things

A Nice House   Loving Parents

Many Friends

A Lot of Toys   Good Health

Good Grades   Cool Clothes

Which of the seven items shown above is the **most** important in your life?

Which is the **least** important?

Rank the list in order of importance to you.

Name _____

The Most Important Things

Circle your answer to each question below. Then explain your choices.

1. Which would you rather do on Saturday morning? **watch TV / play outside**

_____

2. Which do you prefer for dessert? **store-bought cookies / homemade cookies**

_____

3. Which is more important to you? **getting good grades / being a good athlete**

_____

4. Which do you prefer? **one best friend / many good friends**

_____

Prioritize each list below by numbering **1** to **6**, with **1** as your top priority.
Under "Reasons," write the thoughts that led to your decisions.

Your favorite vacation spot:	**Reasons:**
____ beach	
____ mountains	_____
____ big city	
____ relative's house	_____
____ amusement park	
____ home	_____

Your favorite subject in school:	**Reasons:**
____ reading and language	
____ health	_____
____ math	
____ science	_____
____ social studies	
____ art	_____

Thinking Skills • EMC 5302

What Equipment Will We Need?

Introducing the Skill

It is likely that your students will have had previous experience with Venn diagrams. If not, begin with some concrete experiences before doing the chart and activity page. Create the overlapping circles on the floor, using ropes or string. Use the students themselves for classifying.

For example, label the circles:

- *Boys* and *Students with Tennis Shoes*

- *Students with Brown Eyes* and *Students with Red Hair*

- *Students Wearing Jeans* and *Students Wearing Sweatshirts*

Using the Chart

Use the blackline chart provided in this book or download the interactive version. (See page 3.)

1. Tell students that some games are played with a ball, some with a net, some with both a net and a ball, and some with neither.

2. Show Chart 8.

3. Read the list of games and decide where each game should be placed on the diagram. If you are using the interactive chart, drag the name of each piece of equipment into the correct area of the Venn diagram.

Practicing the Skill

1. Post a world map in the classroom, or have a globe available for reference.

2. Students complete the activity page, *Where in the World?*, on page 105.

Extending the Skill

Have students label their own two-circle diagrams and create lists of items. Then have students ask classmates to classify their items.

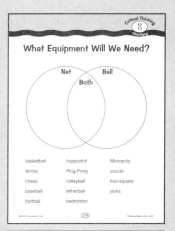

What Equipment Will We Need?

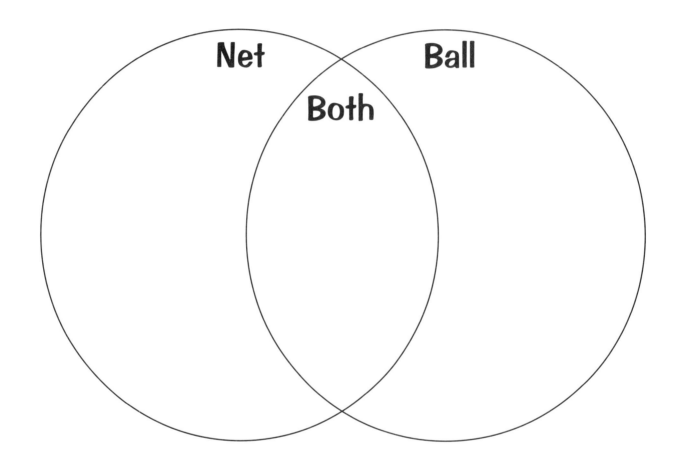

Net   Ball

Both

basketball   hopscotch   Monopoly

tennis   Ping-Pong   soccer

chess   volleyball   four-square

baseball   tetherball   jacks

football   badminton

Thinking Skills • EMC 5302

Name _____

Where in the World?

Use a globe or a world map and the Venn diagram below to organize the names of the continents by the hemisphere in which they lie. Notice that the two circles overlap. List the names of the continents that are in **both** hemispheres in this section.

The Continents

Australia   Antarctica   North America   South America

Asia   Europe   Africa

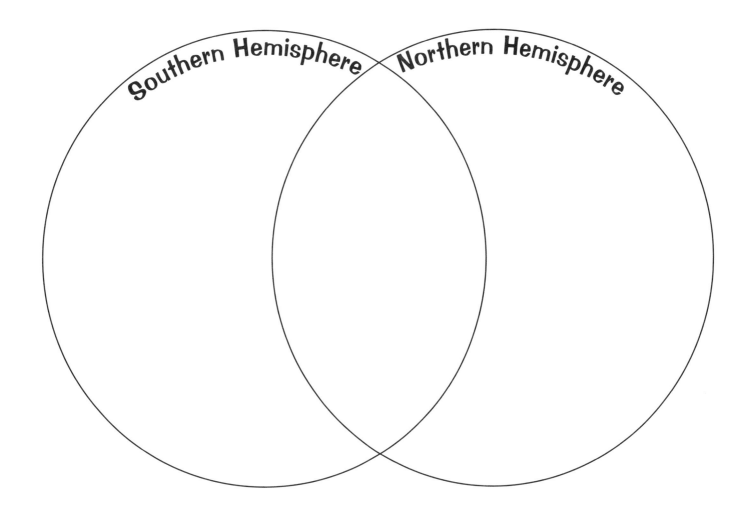

Favorite Flavors

Introducing the Skill

Have students practice drawing overlapping Venn circles before they work independently. They can trace around circular objects or patterns, or use a compass.

Using the Chart

Use the blackline chart provided in this book or download the interactive version. (See page 3.)

1. Show Chart 9.

2. Read the following information:

   Alice is planning an ice-cream feast for her skating club. She decided to buy three flavors of ice cream. She asked the members of her club which of the three flavors they liked. She made a Venn diagram to show their responses. List the name of each club member in the section of the diagram that shows that person's choice(s).

3. Read and discuss the clues with your class. Decide together where each name should be written.

   If you are using the interactive chart, click in a section of the diagram and keyboard the club member name(s) in that section.

Practicing the Skill

1. Students draw a three-circle Venn diagram and complete the activity page, *Hobby Clubs,* on page 108.

2. Remind students that everyone in Ms. Barker's class could join more than one club. Sally could choose the Pet Club or the Collectors Club. Ralph could be listed under Soccer or Soccer and Pets.

Extending the Skill

1. Brainstorm a list of your students' favorite activities on the chalkboard or overhead projector.

2. Have students choose three of the activities, draw a Venn diagram, and label the diagram with those activities.

3. Then have students interview classmates and write their names in the appropriate sections of the diagram. Explain that if interviewed students do <u>not</u> like any of the activities, their names should be written outside the circles.

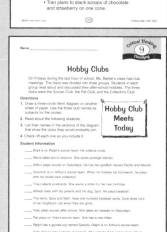

Favorite Flavors

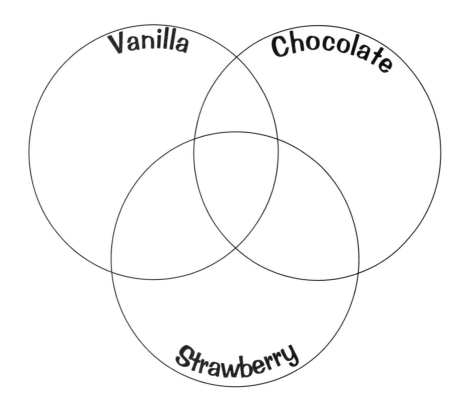

- Alice likes chocolate and strawberry.

- Yoko wants chocolate ice cream and syrup.

- Frank likes strawberry.

- Bill will only eat vanilla.

- Sue likes all three flavors together.

- Mark wants a strawberry-vanilla swirl.

- Eleanor likes chocolate and vanilla.

- Andy won't come if he can't have chocolate.

- Tran plans to stack scoops of chocolate
  and strawberry on one cone.

Thinking Skills • EMC 5302

Hobby Clubs

On Fridays during the last hour of school, Ms. Barker's class had club meetings. The class was divided into three groups. Students in each group read about and discussed their after-school hobbies. The three clubs were the Soccer Club, the Pet Club, and the Collectors Club.

Directions

1. Draw a three-circle Venn diagram on another sheet of paper. Use the three club names as subjects for the circles.

2. Read about the following students.

3. List their names in the sections of the diagram that show the clubs they would probably join.

4. Check off each one as you include it.

Student Information

_____ Brad is on Ralph's soccer team. He collects rocks.

_____ Maria takes tennis lessons. She saves postage stamps.

_____ Arthur plays soccer on Saturdays. He has two goldfish named Pacific and Atlantic.

_____ Solomon is on Arthur's soccer team. When he finishes his homework, he plays with his model train collection.

_____ Tina collects postcards. She wants a kitten for her next birthday.

_____ Alfredo lives with his parents and his dog, Spot. He plays baseball.

_____ The twins, Sara and Seth, have one hundred baseball cards. Sara takes care of her neighbors' cat when they are gone.

_____ Yoko plays soccer after school. She takes art classes on Saturdays.

_____ Pat plays on Yoko's soccer team. She has a new kitten.

_____ Ralph has a guinea pig named Speedy. Ralph is on Arthur's soccer team.

_____ Sally likes to take pictures of animals. She collects them in her photo album.

Treasure Map

Introducing the Skill

This map grid is a good beginning step in using a compass rose and moving in specific directions and distances on a map.

Using the Chart

Use the blackline chart provided in this book or download the interactive version. (See page 3.)

1. Show Chart 10.

2. If your students are unfamiliar with a compass rose, point it out and explain what it means.

3. Explain that when students stop in a square on the map grid, they will collect the letter in that square. They should write down the letters in order to find out who hid the treasure.

4. Provide students with a copy of the following directions, or have students listen and follow directions as you read. If you are using the interactive chart, click in each square to move across the map. Note that the letters collected will appear on the lines as you click in the squares.

   1. *Begin at the hut in the upper-left corner, and travel three squares southeast.*

   2. *Now go two squares north.*

   3. *Continue across the river, three squares east.*

   4. *Then go five squares southwest.*

   5. *Travel on, four squares north.*

   6. *Walk through the meadow, three squares east.*

   7. *Go three squares southwest.*

   8. *March five squares due east.*

   9. *Move two squares north.*

   10. *Finally, hike down to the treasure, buried three squares southwest.*

Practicing the Skill

Students complete the activity page, *Find Tony's House,* on page 111.

Treasure Map

A pirate found himself stranded on an island with a huge chest of gold. He buried the gold and drew this map.

Find the treasure and learn who hid it.

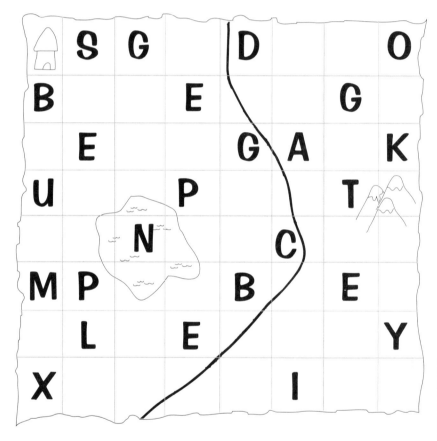

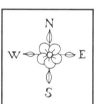

Who hid the treasure?

_____ _____ _____   _____ _____ _____

_____ _____   _____ _____

Thinking Skills • EMC 5302

Name _____

Find Tony's House

Tony sent you an invitation to his birthday party. He lives in a subdivision where all the houses look alike, so he included this list of clues. Use the list and the map to find Tony's house. Draw a balloon on Tony's door to help other partygoers find the right spot.

Clues:

1. Go three squares southeast.

2. Move two squares north.

3. Turn west and go one square.

4. Run two squares south.

5. Go southwest one square.

6. Move three squares east.

7. Two squares north and you're at Tony's house!

What Do You Need to Know?

Introducing the Skill

Relevant details give the reader information that he or she needs to make a decision. Irrelevant details are not connected to the matter at hand. Students need to evaluate the details they are given when they are playing a game or making a decision, as well as when they are reading.

Using the Chart

Use the blackline chart provided in this book or download the interactive version. (See page 3.)

1. Show Chart 11.

2. Discuss the chart and ask students to name details that are relevant, or important, to their playing in a baseball game. *(Relevant details: when the game will take place, where the game will take place, what position you will play, and how the game is played.)*

3. Have students name the irrelevant details. If you are using the interactive chart, click on the question marks to reveal the word *relevant* or *irrelevant. (Irrelevant details: what the team mascot is, where the coach is from, and who the officials are.)*

Practicing the Skill

Students complete the activity page, *What's Important?,* on page 114.

Extending the Skill

Reinforce the meaning of the terms **relevant** and **irrelevant** on a daily basis. For example, discuss with students how a particular lesson can be relevant to their lives, both today and in the future. This discussion may lead to some lively classroom discourse on the relevance of specific academic skills.

What Do You Need to Know?

If you are planning on playing in a baseball game, which of the following details are important for you to know?

1. when the game will take place

2. what the team mascot is

3. where the game will take place

4. what position you will play

5. where the coach is from

6. who the officials are

7. how the game is played

 Thinking Skills • EMC 5302

Name _____

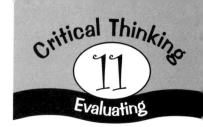

What's Important?

In each situation below, decide which details are relevant.
Circle **all** the relevant details for each situation.

1. You are going to a party.

- who is going to be there
- what the date of the party is
- what time the party starts
- what foods will be served
- what you are supposed to bring

2. You are making a chocolate cake.

- what temperature the oven needs to be
- who likes chocolate cake
- what ingredients you use
- how long the cake needs to bake
- who gets the first piece

3. You are having a social studies test.

- what material the test covers
- the number of questions on the math test
- what type of test it will be
- your score on the last social studies test
- when the test is scheduled

Now try these on your own.

4. What details are **relevant** to buying your mother a birthday present?

_____

_____

5. What details are **irrelevant** to choosing a best friend?

_____

_____

Lucky Shoes

Introducing the Skill

Observation is an important skill. Observing a photograph or an illustration is different than observing a real object.

Using the Chart

Use the blackline chart provided in this book or download the interactive version. (See page 3.)

1. Show Chart 12.

2. Record several of the students' descriptions of Coach Brown's missing shoes and save them for comparison with the following observation.

   If you are using the interactive chart, click in the text box to keyboard the description.

3. Provide a pair of real shoes. Review with students the five senses that are used for observation. Encourage them to use more than just their sense of sight to describe the real shoes.

   How do the shoes look?
   How do the shoes feel?
   How do the shoes smell?
   How do the shoes sound?

4. Reread the descriptions of Coach Brown's shoes and compare them with the descriptions of the real shoes. Ask students, *Which description is more complete? Why?*

Practicing the Skill

Students complete the activity page, *Look Closely,* on page 117.

Extending the Skill

To reinforce the concept of using the five senses in observation, have students play this modified version of Twenty Questions.

1. Make a set of index cards with the name of one ordinary object on each card *(e.g., clock, tissue box, math book, garden hose, hammer).*

2. Ask a volunteer leader to choose one card, read the word, and keep it a secret.

3. Have students ask the leader 20 questions about the object that can only be answered *yes* or *no.* If no one guesses, the leader furnishes the answer, and then a new leader continues the game.

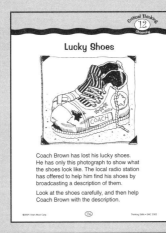

Lucky Shoes

Coach Brown has lost his lucky shoes. He has only this photograph to show what the shoes look like. The local radio station has offered to help him find his shoes by broadcasting a description of them.

Look at the shoes carefully, and then help Coach Brown with the description.

 # Look Closely

Read each set of clues about ordinary objects.
Draw a picture of each object that is being described and label it.

1. This object can be found in the classroom. It is shaped like a very small cylinder, but it is not hollow. It can be short or long. Most commonly, it is white or yellow. It feels smooth and silky to the touch, usually with a rounded edge on one end and a straight edge on the other. If you tasted it, it might be bitter. It has a dusty smell. When used, this object makes scratchy noises. Sometimes it squeaks and squeals.

2. This object can be found in the kitchen or garage. The top part of this object is a long, skinny stick. It can be any color. It feels smooth to the touch. The bottom part is made of many bristles tied together. It is usually pale yellow in color. The end of it feels sharp and prickly. It smells fresh and outdoorsy, like a newly mowed field. It has no taste. When used, it makes a swishing sound.

3. This object can be found in any building or home. It is usually round in shape and is a little smaller than a baseball. Usually it is gold or silver, but it can be clear or white. It feels smooth and cool to the touch. It can be turned both clockwise and counterclockwise when handled. When turned, it may make clicking sounds. It has no smell or taste.

(117) Thinking Skills • EMC 5302

My Coat

Introducing the Skill

1. With a permanent marker, write sequential numbers on the potatoes in a bag of baking potatoes.

2. Give each student one potato. Have students carefully observe all the details about their potatoes. Record the number of the potato each student has observed.

3. Divide the class into four groups. Have each group place their potatoes in an opaque bag or a box.

4. Give each student in each group 30 seconds to find his or her potato by feeling the potatoes in the bag. Check the number and return the potato to the bag before the next student takes a turn.

Using the Chart

Use the blackline chart provided in this book or download the interactive version. (See page 3.)

1. Show Chart 13.

2. Give students time to think about how they would describe their coats. If you are using the interactive chart, click in the text box to keyboard the description.

3. Have students share descriptions with partners.

4. Ask students how they remembered some or all of the details about their coats. *(Some might say that they could visualize the coat in their heads. Some might remember colors, and others the way it feels. Some may not remember any details.)*

Practicing the Skill

Students complete the activity page, *Testing Your Powers,* on page 120.

Extending the Skill

Sharpen students' visual powers by playing this version of I Spy.

1. Ask a selected volunteer to secretly choose a mystery person and call out, *I spy someone who is _____. (two- or three-word general description—a tall boy, a short girl)*

2. Have the class ask five questions about the physical attributes of the mystery person. The questions may only be answered *yes* or *no*. The person who guesses the mystery person then becomes the new leader.

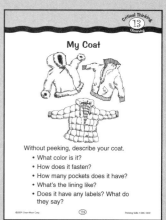

My Coat

Without peeking, describe your coat.

- What color is it?

- How does it fasten?

- How many pockets does it have?

- What's the lining like?

- Does it have any labels? What do they say?

Name _____

Testing Your Powers

Test your powers of observation and memory by answering the following questions. Leave blank any questions you can't answer.

1. Without peeking, what is the color of your teacher's eyes?

_____

2. What did you eat for dinner last night?

_____

3. What did your teacher wear to school yesterday?

_____

4. On what day of the week was your last birthday?

_____

5. How many outside doors are there in your school?

_____

6. What game did you play at recess or in P.E. class yesterday?

_____

7. What is the name of someone on the school custodial staff?

_____

8. What is the name of your teacher from last year?

_____

Puzzling the Planets

Introducing the Skill

Looking for similarities and differences in words, numbers, and figures tests students' power of observation. Having them distinguish between similar-looking words and numbers teaches students to pay close attention to detail. Utilizing this skill enables students to perform better on standardized tests, which often contain multiple-choice items of similar nature. Looking closely for similarities and differences also improves students' spelling and general reading abilities.

Using the Chart

Use the blackline chart provided in this book or download the interactive version. (See page 3.)

1. Show Chart 14.

2. Have students follow the clues on the chart to find the answer to the question.

3. If you are using the interactive chart, click on a planet to check whether your answer is correct.

Practicing the Skill

Students complete the activity page, *Space Quiz,* on page 123.

Extending the Skill

1. Have students write *tram* on their papers.

2. Tell them to change one letter to make a new word that tells what a waiter uses to carry plates of food. *(tray)*

3. Tell them to change one letter to make a new word that tells the color of an elephant. *(gray)*

4. Tell them to change one letter to make a new word that is a unit of weight. *(gram)*

5. Tell them to change one letter to make a new word that is very gloomy. *(grim)*

Puzzling the Planets

Which planet in our solar system is the most like Earth? Follow the clues to find the correct answer.

- The first letter appears in **groom**, not **grown**.

- The next letter appears in **east**, not **west**.

- The third letter appears in **brought**, not **bought**.

- The last letter appears in **sew**, not **few**.

Thinking Skills • EMC 5302

Space Quiz

Work through each set of clues below and write your answers on the lines.

1. Stephen is looking for the name of the planet that is sixth from the sun.

   The first letter appears in **faster**, not **father**.
   The next letter appears in **paper**, not **proper**.
   The third letter appears in **west**, not **swell**.
   The fourth letter appears in **shutter**, not **shelter**.
   The fifth letter appears in **near**, not **lean**.
   The last letter appears in **manner**, not **mare**.

   _____ _____ _____ _____ _____ _____

2. Allison wants to know the year that men first landed on Earth's moon.

   The first numeral appears in both **342,198** and **571,605**.
   The second numeral appears in both **34,540,195** and **26,927,886**.
   The third numeral appears in both **691.27** and **835.64**.
   The last numeral appears in both **73,097** and **68,219**.

   _____ _____ _____ _____

3. Emily needs to find the name for a large piece of rock and ice from outer space that orbits the sun in an elliptical path every certain number of years.

   The first letter appears in **mince**, not **ermine**.
   The second letter appears in **drop**, not **pride**.
   The next letter appears in **same**, not **tease**.
   The fourth letter appears in **repeat**, not **trap**.
   The final letter appears in **trash**, not **share**.

   _____ _____ _____ _____ _____

4. On another sheet of paper, write a set of letter clues for your favorite planet or constellation. Ask a classmate to find the answer.

A Long Time Ago Someone Said...

Introducing the Skill

1. Write *It never rains but it pours* on the chalkboard, chart, or overhead projector.

2. Explain that sayings such as this one are called **proverbs**. Say:

   Proverbs are short, wise sayings. They are bits of advice about the way one should live. They don't always mean exactly what the words say. You have to think about the message.

3. Ask students to explain what the proverb means. *(When one unlucky event comes along, sometimes you have a lot more bad luck that comes with it.)*

4. Ask students to give an example of a situation where the proverb might be used. For example:

   Brad fell when he was running to catch the school bus. He tore a hole in his new pants. He went home to change, and missed the bus. He walked the two miles to school and arrived too late for the wildlife assembly. At lunchtime, he discovered that he had left his lunch money in his new pants.

Using the Chart

Use the blackline chart provided in this book or download the interactive version. (See page 3.)

1. Show Chart 15.

2. Discuss the proverbs on the chart as a class. If you are using the interactive chart, click in the text box to keyboard an explanation of each proverb.

Practicing the Skill

1. Leave Chart 15 posted for student reference.

2. Students complete the activity page, *A Long Time Ago Someone Said...,* on page 126.

Extending the Skill

Encourage students to collect proverbs. Look for them in reading and conversations. Have students illustrate the literal meaning and then write an explanation of each proverb.

A Long Time Ago Someone Said...

What do you think these proverbs mean?

A. Birds of a feather flock together.

B. Too many cooks spoil the broth.

C. Every cloud has a silver lining.

D. A stitch in time saves nine.

E. Two heads are better than one.

A Long Time Ago Someone Said...

Each of the following groups of sentences tells about a problem. Match the sentences with the proverb on the chart that offers the best advice or describes the problem.

Write the letter of the proverb on the line next to the situation it matches.

_____ **1.** Beverly couldn't do the problems on her math homework. She thought they were much too difficult. Her brother sat down with her and helped her work the problems.

_____ **2.** Max was disappointed that he couldn't go ice-skating with his friends on Saturday. But then his cousins came to visit in the afternoon and brought their new computer games.

_____ **3.** Alex, Baby Brad, Megan, and Alicia watched their mother make apple pie. When Mother answered the phone, Alex helped by adding a cup of sugar to the apples. When Mother answered the door, Megan added a cup of sugar to the apples. When Mother took the clothes out of the dryer, Alicia lifted Brad up to the counter so he could pour in a cup of sugar, too.

_____ **4.** Pele wanted to show all the members of the art club the award he had won for his painting. He found all of them in the art center, painting a mural for parent night.

_____ **5.** It was Maria's job to mow the lawn. She didn't want to do it before she went to summer camp. When she came home three weeks later, the grass was so long that it took her all day to mow it.

Who Is Right?

Introducing the Skill

1. Write the proverb *Many hands make light work* on the chalkboard or overhead projector.

2. Ask students to give situations where this would be good advice. If they need help getting started, suggest that two or three people helping with the dishes after a big meal might get the work done sooner and easier than only one person.

3. After students have had time to discuss situations where the proverb's advice should be taken, write or project the proverb *Too many cooks spoil the broth*. Ask students to give situations where this proverb would be good advice.

4. Ask students to compare the meaning of the two proverbs.

Using the Chart

Use the blackline chart provided in this book or download the interactive version. (See page 3.)

1. Show Chart 16.

2. As a class, discuss the meaning of the pairs of proverbs.

3. If you are using the interactive chart, click on a pair of proverbs to focus on that pair. Click on the Back button to choose another proverb.

4. Have small groups of students think of an example for each proverb.

Practicing the Skill

Students complete the activity page, *Proverbs,* on page 129.

Extending the Skill

Read Aesop's fables and have the students create a moral or proverb that describes each story. Compare students' answers to the ones given by Aesop.

Thinking Skills • EMC 5302

Who Is Right?

The proverbs in each pair have opposite meanings. Explain what each proverb means. Which one do you think offers the best advice?

> *He who hesitates is lost.*
> *Look before you leap.*

> *Out of sight, out of mind.*
> *Absence makes the heart grow fonder.*

> *Fine clothes make the man.*
> *You can't judge a book by its cover.*

Thinking Skills • EMC 5302

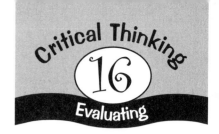

Proverbs

Choose your favorite proverb listed on the chart. Write the proverb on the line below. Then draw pictures that show the meaning of that proverb. Here is an example to get you started:

He who hesitates is lost.

_____

Decisions

Introducing the Skill

Ask students to think about public parks they have used. Ask, *Have you ever noticed any problems? Whose responsibility is it to solve the problems?*

Using the Chart

Use the blackline chart provided in this book or download the interactive version. (See page 3.)

1. Show Chart 17.

2. Divide the class into small groups. Have groups brainstorm and record any possible solutions to the park ranger's problems.

3. As a class, share the responses. Compare the different solutions. Think about how many ideas are the same and how many are different.

4. If you are using the interactive chart, click in the text box to record students' responses.

Practicing the Skill

1. Students complete the activity page, *Decisions,* on page 132.

2. As a class, share the solutions.

Extending the Skill

1. Identify a problem that exists in a public park in your neighborhood or community.

2. Have students brainstorm possible solutions.

3. Then work with students to write a letter to the person(s) responsible for solving the problem, listing their suggestions.

Decisions

Bonny, the park ranger, takes care of the animals and visitors in Bearville State Park.

She needs your help. Study the picture.

What should Bonny do to solve the problem?

Decisions

Bonny, the park ranger, would like your advice. She needs help with these problems in Bearville State Park. What do you think she should do? Write as many ideas as you can.

1. On Sundays, too many people come to Bearville State Park. There aren't enough parking spaces, so people leave their cars everywhere.

_____

_____

_____

_____

2. People like to see the bears. Even though there are signs everywhere that say, "Don't Feed the Animals," people still offer them food.

_____

_____

_____

_____

3. Many campers coming to Bearville State Park want to learn more about the wild animals that live there. On weekends, Bonny spends so much time answering questions that she doesn't have time to patrol the park.

_____

_____

_____

_____

Thinking Skills • EMC 5302

It's Your Choice

Introducing the Skill

1. Begin by letting students know that everyone, even teachers, make mistakes. A real-life example of a real mistake you have made might be a good addition to the discussion.

2. Ask students what they do when they make a mistake.

Using the Chart

Use the blackline chart provided in this book or download the interactive version. (See page 3.)

1. Show Chart 18.

2. Have students look at the sequence of events on the chart and identify the problem.

3. Have each student give an opinion about what Jason should do.

4. If you are using the interactive chart, click in the text box to record students' responses.

Practicing the Skill

1. Have students consider the effect that other people's requests have on their decisions. Ask, *Have you ever changed your plans because of someone else's request?*

2. Students complete the activity page, *What Will You Do?,* on page 135.

   Note: If the writing task is too difficult for your students, divide the class into small groups. Give one problem to each group, and allow time for them to discuss the situation and agree on a solution. Then have groups present their problem and solution.

Extending the Skill

Have each student cite a situation from his or her own experiences that is similar to the situation on the activity page. Pose the situations to the class, and have students respond as advice columnists with possible solutions.

It's Your Choice

Jason has a problem.
What should he do?

 **What Will You Do?**

Sometimes you have to make decisions that change your plans.
Read the following stories and decide what you should do.

1. Mrs. James calls you on Tuesday. She needs a baby sitter for Thursday
   afternoon. She knows it's a school night, so she'll be home by 7:30. You
   have a science report due on Friday. You had planned to work on the
   report Thursday afternoon.

   _____

   _____

2. Your little sister wants to go skating in the park on Saturday. Your mother
   asks you to go with her. You had planned to spend the day at a friend's
   house.

   _____

   _____

3. Your aunt gave you a new bicycle and helmet for your birthday two weeks
   ago. It's been raining, so you haven't been able to ride it. Your brother has
   a bicycle, but his helmet is too small. He wants to borrow the helmet on
   Saturday so he can go on a bicycle trip with his nature club. It's his birthday.
   You had planned to ride your bicycle to meet your friends for basketball
   practice. Your mother won't let you ride your bicycle without your helmet.

   _____

   _____

Pulley Puzzle

Introducing the Skill

1. If your students are unfamiliar with pulleys, set up a model to show how a pulley works. Ask your custodian to loan you one, buy an inexpensive one at a hardware store, or make one using a wooden spool and a wire bent into a triangle.

2. Thread a lightweight rope or string through the pulley.

3. Tie identical containers (small baskets, yogurt cups, boxes) to each end of the rope.

4. Have students place marbles or Unifix® cubes in the containers. (Students should soon discover that the heavier container lifts the lighter container.)

Using the Chart

Use the blackline chart provided in this book or download the interactive version. (See page 3.)

1. Show Chart 19.

2. Have students identify the pulley that is not working correctly. Be sure to have them explain why they chose the pulley that they did.

3. If you are using the interactive chart, click on the pulleys to check your answers.

Practicing the Skill

Students complete the activity page, *Another Pulley Puzzle,* on page 138.

Extending the Skill

Set up a pulley center in your classroom. Have students manipulate different objects and record the results of their experiments.

Pulley Puzzle

The children on these ropes weigh exactly the same amount, and the monkey weighs less than a child. Which pulley is **not** working correctly?

Another Pulley Puzzle

Can you balance each of the pulleys? Cut out the pulleys and the objects. Place all of the objects on the three pulley systems so that each system is balanced.

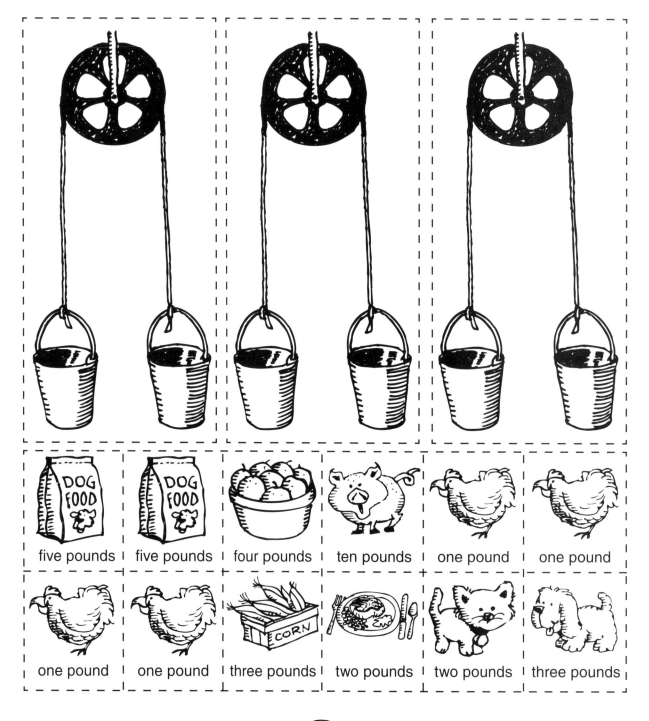

five pounds | five pounds | four pounds | ten pounds | one pound | one pound

one pound | one pound | three pounds | two pounds | two pounds | three pounds

Thinking Skills • EMC 5302

Answer Key

Chart 8

Creative Thinking

Chart 1
Answers will vary.

Activity Page 7
Answers will vary.

Chart 2
Some possible new uses for a transformed toothbrush may include: a push broom, a rake, a mop, a pipe cleaner, a bottle cleaner, a bracelet that cleans computer and piano keyboards, and on and on.

Activity Page 10
Answers will vary.

Chart 3
Answers will vary.

Activity Page 13
Answers will vary.

Chart 4
Answers will vary.

Activity Page 16
Answers will vary.

Chart 5
You are at a circus. The man is a clown.

Activity Page 19
Paragraphs will vary.

Chart 6
Some moms are short. Some moms are tall. But you're the BEST mom of all.

Activity Page 22
Answers will vary.

Chart 7
Students' responses will vary.

Activity Page 25
Descriptions will vary.

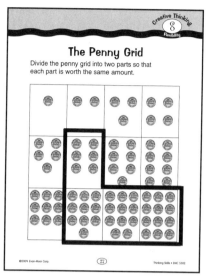

Each section contains 39 cents.

Activity Page 28

Chart 9
The chart is used in conjunction with the worksheet. There are 9 possible ways to arrange the scoops with chocolate as the first scoop.

Activity Page 31
There are 27 possible ways to arrange the scoops with 3 flavors of ice cream.

Logical Thinking

Chart 1
The Hopi blanket has three different stripes that repeat in an ABCB pattern. The Arapaho blanket has four stripes that repeat in an ABAC pattern if you look at color only. If you begin with white and use color and size of stripe, the pattern is ABCB. The Navajo blanket has two stripes that repeat in an AB pattern.

Activity Page 35
Each of the three sections of the hat has its own repeating pattern. The ninth hat should look like this:

 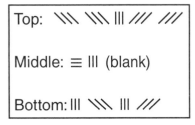

Top: \\\ \\\ ||| /// ///

Middle: ≡ ||| (blank)

Bottom: ||| \\\ ||| ///

Chart 2
Opposite pairs from the chart are: first and last (1, 4); sweet and sour (7, 3); summer and winter (8, 6); front and back (2, 5).

Activity Page 38
Any combinations with the opposite pairs listed on the student page are acceptable because all of the pairs are opposites.

Chart 3
1. Anything that would be stored in a cupboard: a plate, a computer, a book, etc.
2. bird
3. hand
4. fish

Activity Page 41
1. C   3. A
2. B   4. C

Chart 4
1. cat   4. rug
2. bird   5. feet
3. feathers   6. cry

Activity Page 44
1. smell : nose :: hear : ear
2. cub : bear :: chick : hen
3. air : sky :: water : ocean

Original analogies will vary.

Chart 5
Accept any reasonable answer, such as: Horses were an important way to travel. Horses helped people travel. Horses were a chief form of transportation in the 1800s.

Activity Page 47
Accept all reasonable answers, such as: Pioneers had fun helping each other. Pioneers found time for fun by holding work parties.

Chart 6
Ostriches and swans both have long necks. Ostriches are larger than swans; ostriches are brown, and swans are white or black, etc. Giraffes are not birds just because they have long necks.

Activity Page 50
1. F
2. T
3. F
4. F
5. a dime can be used for money.
6. beetles have six legs and three body parts.

Chart 7
Edward's last name is Smith. The syllogism is valid.

Activity Page 53
1. b
2. c
3. c
4. a

Chart 8

1. All monsters have big, sharp teeth.
   All giants are monsters.
   Therefore, all giants have big, sharp teeth.

2. All butterflies are flying to the moon.
   All monarchs are butterflies.
   Therefore, all monarchs are flying to the moon.

3. No cars have wings.
   Some machines are cars.
   Therefore, some machines do not have wings.

Activity Page 56

Syllogisms 1 and 4 are invalid.

Chart 9

Spot ate the peanut butter cookie and Sara ate the chocolate chip cookies.

Activity Page 59

Edward's favorite is bean; Lisa's favorite is vegetable; Ben's favorite is chicken noodle; and Lara's favorite is tomato.

Chart 10

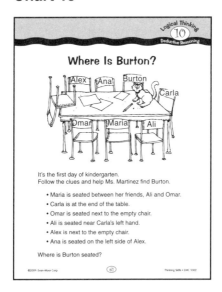

Activity Page 62

A–Fix-It Hardware; B–Food! Food!;
C–Shoe Tree; D–Animal Barn;
E–Young's Yummy Yogurt; F–Delicious Deli;
G–Fancy Duds; H–Star Theater

Chart 11

Directions will vary.

Activity Page 65

Answers will vary.

Chart 12

103: Ivan–Ivan is building a giant sandbox.
104: Maurice–Maurice is working on a skateboard jump.
105: Carmen–Carmen is digging a fishpond.
106: Tom–Tom is hanging a new tire swing.
107: Breanne–Breanne is building a fort.

Activity Page 68

left to right: Jose, Nga, Sabrina, Alex

Chart 13

Alicia—Log Ride; Ann—Roller Coaster; Hernaldo—Jungle Ride; Rachel—Sky Ride; Raul—Ferris Wheel; Tim—Wild Thing

Activity Page 71

Arlene—Fido the turtle
Carlos—Tom the cat
Cecelia—Dipsey the rabbit
Chad—Rascal the dog
Juan—Curly the snake
Nancy—Smiley the fish

Chart 14

36, 28, 33, 25
The pattern is +5, −8.

Activity Page 74

A. 15, 10, 6; pattern: −9, −8, −7, −6, −5, −4, etc.

B. 3, 5, 4; pattern: −1, +2

C. 36, 49; pattern: "squares"
   (2 x 2, 3 x 3, 4 x 4, 5 x 5, 6 x 6, 7 x 7)
   or +5, +7, +9, +11, +13, etc.

D. 406, 507; pattern: add 1 to the number in the hundreds place and 1 to the number in the ones place **or** add 101

E. 576, 687; pattern: add 1 to the number in the hundreds place, add 1 to the number in the tens place, and add 1 to the number in the ones place **or** add 111

Chart 15

First bed: top—Pete or Igor
            bottom—Ted or Sam

Second bed: top—Ben
               bottom—Franz

Third bed: top—Fred
              bottom—Nate

Fourth bed: top—Hernando
               bottom—Ed

Fifth bed: top—Igor or Pete
             bottom—Sam or Ted

Activity Page 77
This page is used in conjunction with the chart.

Chart 16
15 triangles

Activity Page 80
The largest possible triangle is 7 triangles high from base to apex. It contains 118 triangles. Answers will vary if students do not cut the largest possible triangle. In that case, have students with the same sized triangles compare answers.

Critical Thinking

Chart 1
Only the first one in the last row is a Curly Q.

Activity Page 84
Answers will vary. The Cool Dog drawn must have a hat, a collar, and a long tail.

Chart 2
Answers will vary and might include: short, rounded heads with erect ears; large eyes with vertical-slit pupils; large, strong fangs; and retractable claws.

Activity Page 87
All the vehicles share these attributes: wheels, gears, a steering device, and a place for the driver to sit.

Chart 3
The fish is different. They are all living things, they have tails, they hunt for food, etc. Membership to the Animal Club depends on having four feet and breathing with lungs.

Activity Page 90
1. bear (others are in the cat family)

2. coffee (others are white)

3. Two answers are possible: diamond (others have curved lines) **or** S (others are closed figures).

4. arrow with dot (other shapes surround the dot or are closed figures)

5. pine (others are flowers)

6. rectangle with three lines (others have 4 projections sticking out from the shape)

Chart 4
The car doesn't belong because it is not a symbol related to a holiday. The remaining picture can be classified as holiday symbols.

Activity Page 93
1. easel, circus

2. bus, farm

3. capitalization, mathematics

4. neighing, moving

5. arms, organs

6. presidents' names

7. ways to proceed when driving **or** traffic commands

8. dairy products

9. Answers will vary.

10. Answers will vary.

Chart 5
1. spoon/dishes

2. horse/young animals

3. cookies/beverages

4. table/furniture to sit on

Activity Page 96

1. paper/used on paper to write or paint
2. TV/printed reading materials
3. furniture polish/used to clean floors
4. circle/figures with straight lines
5. underwear/outer clothing
6. roof/inside parts of the house
7. lake/moving waterways

Chart 6

By height to shoulder: elephant, giraffe, rhinoceros, aardvark and musk deer (both have same height to shoulder), shrew. If compared by head-to-toe height, the giraffe is the tallest.

By weight: elephant, rhinoceros, giraffe, aardvark, musk deer, shrew

By length: elephant, rhinoceros, giraffe, aardvark, musk deer, shrew

Activity Page 99

Any reasonable categories are acceptable. Possible answers: large/small; tusks/no tusks; herbivorous/carnivorous; horns/no horns; African/American/Asian

Chart 7

Answers will vary.

Activity Page 102

Answers will vary.

Chart 8

Net—badminton; **Both**—Ping-Pong, volleyball, tennis, basketball, soccer; **Ball**—four-square, jacks, football, tetherball, baseball; **Neither**—Monopoly, hopscotch, chess

Activity Page 105

Southern Hemisphere—Antarctica, Australia
Northern Hemisphere—North America, Europe, Asia
Both—Africa, South America

Chart 9

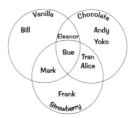

Activity Page 108

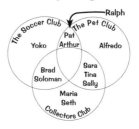

Chart 10

Peg-Leg Pete

Activity Page 111

Name ______________________

Critical Thinking 10 Problem Solving

Find Tony's House

Tony sent you an invitation to his birthday party. He lives in a subdivision where all the houses look alike, so he included this list of clues. Use the list and the map to find Tony's house. Draw a balloon on Tony's door to help other partygoers find the right spot.

Clues:
1. Go three squares southeast.
2. Move two squares north.
3. Turn west and go one square.
4. Run two squares south.
5. Go southwest one square.
6. Move three squares east.
7. Two squares north and you're at Tony's house!

Start Here

©2009 Evan-Moor Corp. 111 Thinking Skills • EMC 5302

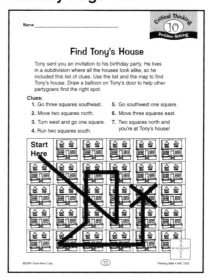

Chart 11

Relevant details: when the game will take place; where the game will take place; what position you will play; how the game is played.
Irrelevant details: what the team mascot is; where the coach is from; and who the officials are.

Activity Page 114

1. what the date of the party is, what time the party starts, what you are supposed to bring

2. what temperature the oven needs to be, what ingredients you use, how long the cake needs to bake

3. what material the test covers, what type of test it will be, when the test is scheduled

4. Answers will vary.

5. Answers will vary.

Chart 12
Descriptions will vary.

Activity Page 117

1. chalk

2. broom

3. doorknob

Chart 13
Answers will vary.

Activity Page 120
Answers will vary.

Chart 14
Mars

Activity Page 123

1. The sixth planet from the sun is **Saturn**.

2. The year men first landed on the moon was **1969**.

3. A large piece of rock and ice that orbits the sun is a **comet**.

4. Answers will vary.

Chart 15

A. People tend to associate with others who are like themselves.

B. When too many people get involved in a project, it doesn't turn out well.

C. An unpleasant event (the cloud) often has something good (the silver lining) that comes with it.

D. Take care of a problem right away or it may get worse.

E. Problems are more easily solved when people work together.

Activity Page 126

1. E	4. A
2. C	5. D
3. B	

Chart 16
Pair 1
If you delay too long before acting, you may miss an opportunity.
Be cautious; know what you're getting into before you act.

Pair 2
When a person isn't around, we forget about him/her.
We often think we like someone more after the person has gone away.

Pair 3
The clothes a person chooses to wear determines the person he/she is.
What a person looks like doesn't define what kind of a person he/she is.

Activity Page 129
Answers will vary.

Chart 17
Answers will vary.

Activity Page 132
Answers will vary.

Chart 18
Answers will vary.

Activity Page 135
Answers will vary.

Chart 19
The incorrect pulley is number 3; it shows the monkey down and the child up.

Activity Page 138
There are many correct solutions.

One example:

Pulley 1—left side = dog food + chicken
right side = puppy + corn

Pulley 2—left side = pig
right side = dog food + apples + chicken

Pulley 3—left side = kitten + chicken
right side = lunch + chicken